CAPITAL PUNISHMENT

CAPITAL PUNISHMENT

CRIMINAL LAW AND SOCIAL EVOLUTION

JAN GORECKI

COLUMBIA UNIVERSITY PRESS
NEW YORK

The translation of an excerpt of Pericles' funeral oration has been reprinted from: Karl R. Popper, *The Open Society and its Enemies* (Princeton University Press, 5th rev. edn., 1966, reprinted 1980, and Routledge and Kegan Paul, 5th rev. edn., 1966, reprinted 1980). Copyright © 1962, 1966 by Karl Raimund Popper. Reprinted by permission of Sir Karl Popper, Princeton University Press, and Routledge and Kegan Paul.

Library of Congress Cataloging in Publication Data

Górecki, Jan.
  Capital punishment.

  Bibliography: p.
  Includes index.
  1. Capital punishment—United States.
2. Capital punishment. I. Title.
KF9227.C2G67 1983   364.6′6′0973   83-1875
ISBN 0-231-05658-3

Columbia University Press
New York Guildford, Surrey

c 10 9 8 7 6 5 4 3 2

Clothbound editions of Columbia University Press books are Smyth-sewn and printed on permanent and durable acid-free paper.

To the memory of my Teachers
Jan Gwiazdomorski and Jerzy Lande

CONTENTS

PREFACE

Capital punishment is today among the most controversial problems in America. On the one hand, the heat of the controversy exceeds the weight of the problem; as is pointed out in this book, it is not the presence or absence of capital punishment but other legal reforms that are essential for effective functioning of the criminal justice system in this country. On the other hand, however, whether we send criminals to the gallows presents a moral dilemma of utmost importance.

Owing to the heat of the controversy, recommendations abound both for and against retaining the death penalty. This book does not explicitly support either of these stands; the purpose here is to understand rather than to recommend. More specifically, the purpose is to analyze and explain what has occurred to the death penalty in the United States and to anticipate cautiously what may occur in the future. This does not, however, mean that the book is void of practical implications. If a reader accepts the analysis and explanation to be offered, he may, and probably will, be aided in accepting a stand on what the legal system should do—abolish the death penalty or retain it.

The book starts with a brief analysis of the law of capital punishment. It is a vacillating and confused law, recently shifting from near-abolition to retention. Its development is influenced by a clash of two conflicting forces—the general tendency of social evolution toward milder criminal sanctions and the increasingly punitive attitudes in America today. These two forces are scrutinized and accounted for in the second and third parts of the book. The scrutiny not only explains the development of the law but also throws some light on the future of the death penalty in America.

ACKNOWLEDGMENTS

My thanks are due to Hugo A. Bedau, Professor of Philosophy at Tufts University, for his useful comments. I am also truly indebted to Charles P. Webel and Leslie Bialler, of Columbia University Press, for their most helpful editorial assistance.

Jan Gorecki
May 1983

PART ONE

THE LAW

INTRODUCTION

Since the American Revolution, there has always been in this country an ongoing struggle against capital punishment, led by small numbers of particularly sensitive and zealous individuals with Benjamin Rush and Edward Livingston among the forerunners. Their struggle has been successful on a number of issues such as gradually declining catalogs of capital crimes, elimination of mandatory death penalty, and more humane methods of execution. On the ultimate issue, however, of complete elimination of the penalty, their success has always been limited. By the mid-nineteenth century, only three states—Michigan, Rhode Island, and Wisconsin—introduced total (or nearly total)[1] abolition; they were followed, several decades later, by Minnesota and North Dakota. Ten other states accepted abolition in the years 1872–1917, only to restore the penalty promptly; in just one of them—Maine—reabolition followed a few years later.[2] It is easy to account for the lack of broader success; nationwide, the supporters of the total abolition have always constituted a minority.

Since the late 1950s, however, the minority has grown rapidly. This was a period of accelerated cultural change in America, especially of rising humanitarian and egalitarian concerns. Abolitionist groups became well organized, and their arguments gained increasing support. The arguments were an aggregate of old and new reasons for abolition, and the general climate made the old reasons more persuasive and accounted for the spread of the new. Among the former, there was the belief in the sanctity of human life and the basic immorality of killing anyone by the state; there were the claims that executions endanger the innocent, since judicial errors do occur; that they brutalize the society; that capital punishment does not deter better than confinement and is, therefore, unnecessary; and that the pains of the convicts led to execution and the suffering of those who wait on death row are appalling.

The new stress on reeducation of wrongdoers became another reason of importance—the traditional notion of retribution as the major function of criminal law was losing ground in favor of rehabilitation; and execution is both vindictive and precludes making the criminal better. Moreover, a new belief was emerging about the basic innocence of criminals. Its proponents considered crime to be predetermined by social factors such as deprived childhood, inequality, poverty, and discrimination. Since these determinants are beyond the criminal's control, it is difficult to blame him for his behavior and punish him, in particular by death. It was also stressed that, owing to prejudice, the death penalty was unjustly distributed—it was imposed, for the same kind of criminal behavior, with higher frequencies on the black and the poor.

Last but not least, the British provided a strong boost to the abolitionist sentiment in America by both the 1953 Report of the Royal Commission on Capital Punishment and by subsequent abolition in 1965. No wonder the sentiment spread, and the proportion of Americans favoring capital punishment, even for murder, steadily declined—from 68 percent in 1953 to 51 percent in 1960 to 42 percent in 1966.[3] The increasingly rare executions came to a standstill in 1967, and the abolitionists felt their day was coming. They hoped, in particular, that the then activist Supreme Court would strike the penalty down.

CHAPTER 1

FURMAN v. GEORGIA

The Court became immersed in the issue in 1972; in *Furman v. Georgia*[4] it heard, for the first time, arguments on the per se validity of capital punishment. The controversy among the Justices became so intense that nine separate opinions were submitted. Despite discrepancies among each of these opinions, they may be clustered in three categories: abolitionist, strict constructionist, and neutral. The abolitionist Justices considered capital punishment illegal and, moreover, claimed that it should be absent from a good legal system. The strict constructionists insisted that capital punishment was not illegal, but they would have refrained from supporting the penalty if they had been lawmakers. The neutrals left the issue open for future determination.

The abolitionists, Justices Marshall and Brennan, claimed that the death penalty constitutes cruel and unusual punishment under the prohibition of the Eighth Amendment; consequently, it is invalid per se regardless of depravity of the crime committed. To be sure, in the Framers' intent, the Eighth Amendment was aimed at preventing torture, not death. However, Justices Marshall and Brennan have rejected the binding force of the original meaning. They admit the ongoing process of cultural evolution—"the evolving standards of decency that mark the progress of a maturing society"[5]—and they treat the Eighth Amendment as one of those general clauses in the Constitution that warrant flexibility in adapting law to the evolving standards. This adaptive value of the clauses derives precisely from the fact that the meaning of such expressions as "cruel and unusual" (or "due" and "equal" in Due Process and Equal Protection Clauses) changes through time. Because of this change, "a penalty that was permissible at one time . . . is not necessarily permissible today";[6] and this is particularly true of the penalty of death.

Its cruelty was, in *Furman*, understood in a different manner by each of the two abolitionists. Justice Brennan interprets the Eighth Amendment Clause as synonymous with a ban on any penalty that "does not comport with" the fundamental right to "human dignity";[7] he reduces the immorality of capital punishment to infringement of dignity—to the fact that capital punishment is degrading and humiliating. It is, in his view, degrading, because of three characteristics. First, it is extremely severe, and every penalty of extreme severity degrades the person punished and is, therefore, cruel.[8] Second, in the period preceding *Furman*, there had been a steady decline in executions. Their trivial numbers imply arbitrariness, and an arbitrary infliction of any severe penalty is degrading, that is, cruel.[9] Third, all the purposes of capital punishment can be adequately achieved by imprisonment; a severe penalty excessive for the purposes for which it is inflicted "cannot comport with human dignity"[10] and is, again, cruel.[11]

Justice Marshall distinguishes several meanings of "cruel punishment," finding two of them relevant in this case. First, a penalty is cruel if popular moral sentiment abhors it.[12] Second, even if there is no moral indignation, the penalty is cruel if it is either "teleologically excessive"[13] (that is, a less severe penalty would serve the intended purposes equally well) or unnecessary (that is, serves no valid purpose at all).[14] Capital punishment is, for Justice Marshall, cruel under each of the two rubrics.

He lists several conceivable purposes of capital punishment. Two of them—retribution and general deterrence—are often perceived as most important. Justice Marshall identifies the former with vengeance and considers it an illegitimate goal. Thus, if retribution is the sole aim of the death penalty, the penalty, having no valid purpose, is cruel. He also reviews a substantial body of factual data to conclude that capital punishment is necessary neither as a deterrent from crime nor as fulfillment of any other reasonable purpose—for all purposes imprisonment would do. Hence, in his view, "capital punishment serves no purpose that life imprisonment could not serve equally well"; consequently, it is cruel by being excessive.[15]

Secondly, capital punishment is, in Marshall's view, cruel by being abhorrent to the current moral sentiment of America. True, public opinion polls do not necessarily reflect this abhorrence. They would, however, if the American public had known the truth about the death penalty. There is a widespread belief in its utility. The truth is that not only is the penalty purposeless or excessive (in the just stipulated sense), but, moreover, it is discriminatorily imposed against those who are underprivileged, it carries the risk of executing the innocent, it makes a demoralizing sensation of criminal trial, and it precludes achievement of widely accepted aims—reform and treatment of the criminal.[16] Consequently, whichever of the two criteria one applies, capital punishment is unconstitutional.

The validity of these arguments is uneven,[17] but the basic idea underlying the reasoning of both Justices is forceful and may be spelled out in a simple manner. Whether a penalty is cruel reduces eventually to our moral feelings—it is cruel if its harshness or its infringement of dignity arouses our moral outrage. Our forefathers might have felt that capital punishment was morally right. Our experience is, as the reasoning goes, that it is morally outrageous—by destroying human life it inflicts too great a suffering or too great a degradation to ever be just. "Our experience" means here a feeling commonly shared in America today or, at least, a feeling commonly shared by the moral and intellectual elite—by those who are more sensitive and better informed than others.[18]

Against these views of the two Justices, a simple utilitarian counterargument is often produced. True, capital punishment results in severe suffering and loss of life—the wrongs that would be better avoided. However, the use of capital punishment brings, on balance, a greater good. In particular, it saves, through deterrence, more lives than the number of lives lost by execution and thus decreases the total amount of suffering in the society. In rejoinder, the two abolitionists claim that this is not true—that capital punishment either brings no good to anyone or brings only minor gains outweighed by its harmful consequences and, especially, that it does not deter better than less severe penalties do.

The strict constructionists—Justices Blackmun, Burger, Powell, and Rehnquist—offer a different interpretation. They consider the validity of capital punishment as a clear mandate of constitutional law. Both the Fifth and Fourteenth Amendments explicitly acknowledge capital punishment,[19] and this implies that the Cruel and Unusual Punishment Clause does not preclude the penalty of death; otherwise, there would be an obvious contradiction between the prohibition of the penalty by the Clause and its endorsement by the two amendments.[20] Furthermore, the "virtually unquestioned constitutionality of capital punishment" had been admitted by the Court in a long and "unbroken line of precedent,"[21] from 1879[22] to 1971.[23] Hence, the text of the Constitution, as well as *stare decisis*, makes the punishment legitimate.

To be sure, under the impact of changing conditions, the need to outlaw a constitutionally endorsed penalty may emerge. This may happen, in particular, if a general change of moral sentiment makes the penalty unjust, if in the light of new discoveries the penalty appears purposeless, or if, owing to other changes in the social system, inflicting the penalty becomes a bad policy. When this happens, however, the penalty should be removed by lawmakers rather than by the Court. One reason for this is the separation of powers: "in a democratic society legislatures not courts are constituted to respond to . . . the moral values of the people,"[24] to correct "mistaken judgements,"[25] and "to pronounce policy."[26] Another reason is federalism: establishing criminal penalties belongs primarily to the States, and federal judicial power must not be used to cut this right down.[27] True, it is the Court's responsibility to check constitutional soundness of the penalties imposed by both state and federal lawmakers. However, this responsibility should be exercised with utmost restraint; a penalty may not be invalidated, except in the most "extraordinary case."[28]

All this means only that, in *Furman*, the strict constructionists considered capital punishment constitutionally permissible under the law as it is. It does not mean they would have supported the death penalty had they been themselves lawmakers. In particular, no such contingent support was expressed by Justices Powell and Rehnquist. (However, some of Justice Powell's comments implied that, if pressed to take it, he might have opted against the abolition.[29]) Justice Burger claimed: "If we were possessed of legislative power, I would either join with Mr. Justice Brennan and Mr. Justice Marshall or, at the very least, restrict the use of capital punishment to a small category of the most heinous crimes."[30] And Justice Blackmun asserted: "I yield to no one in the depth of my distaste, antipathy, and, indeed, abhorrence for the death penalty . . . . Were I a legislator, I would vote against [it]."[31]

The last group of *Furman* Justices was neutral—they did not take any stand on the per se validity of capital punishment. Instead, they focused on a narrower question—how the defendants in cases at hand had been selected for execution. Their conclusion was that, owing to unbridled jury discretion, the selection process had been arbitrary and capricious and, therefore, unconstitutional; they complained that so was the selection process all over America.

In particular, Justice Douglas denounced as "cruel and unusual" the arbitrary and discriminatory application of capital punishment to the poor and to minorities,[32] and Justice Stewart claimed that, by being imposed rarely and capriciously, death sentences in America "are cruel and unusual in the same way that being struck by lightning is cruel and unusual."[33] The view of the third member of the neutral group, Justice White, concurred partially with these contentions: capital punishment is pronounced only exceptionally, and "there is no meaningful basis for distinguishing the few cases in which it is imposed from the many cases in which it is not." Owing to its rare and arbitrary application, it is useless—it does not effectively perform any deterrent or other function. Being severe as it is, and its severity not being outweighed by any good to anyone, it is cruel and violates the Eighth Amendment.[34]

There is a degree of convergence between these views and the stand of Justices Brennan and Marshall. As indicated earlier, Brennan claimed that the rarity of executions makes them arbitrary; only a few of the many similar cases are singled out for death, and in Marshall's opinion, those few are, for the most part, singled out on a categorical basis by the defendants' being black and poor. To be sure, both abolitionist Justices used, unlike those neutral, the argument of arbitrariness in an indirect manner: for them capital punishment in the *Furman* cases was cruel, since any capital punishment is cruel, and they considered the arbitrariness as only one factor contributing to the general cruelty of all the death penalties. Despite this difference, the partial convergence made it possible to form a majority in the *Furman* case. Five Justices—the abolitionists and the neutrals—agreed that, at least in the cases at hand, capital punishment was "cruel and unusual" and decided to reverse the cases and remand them to the lower courts.

Furman will stand in American legal history as one of the most peculiar decisions for both what it did and what it refrained from doing. It did not resolve the basic problem of validity of capital punishment; the issue was, in 1972, too dubious and controversial. Instead, by answering a narrower question, it banned the death penalty as applied in the cases at hand. This compromise seemed tolerable for all its members. On the one hand, the compromise did not finally ban the death penalty. On the other, those who abhorred the penalty were at least sure that the decision would stop executions of the defendants at hand and of many others on the death row. "Candor compels me to confess," admitted Justice Marshall when opening his *Furman* opinion, "that I am not oblivious to the fact that this is truly a matter of life and death. Not only does it involve the lives of these three petitioners, but those of the almost 600 condemned men and women in this country currently awaiting execution."[35]

Still, the decision was a strange compromise both in its logic and its implications. Its basic tenet consists of an attack against discretion and the resulting arbitrariness in capital cases. However, in this country, wide discretionary powers are not limited to capital crimes. Vested in courts (and in other participants in criminal process, especially prosecutors and police), the powers are enormous in all kinds of criminal dispositions—indeed, they exceed by far those known to any other open society.

This is due to a peculiar combination of historic factors. One seems to be the common law tradition that has never adopted methods of adjudication as rigorous as the "conceptual jurisprudence" developed in much of Europe. The other is our habit of loose—intermittent and inconsistent—application of criminal laws. This habit, which arose in the wake of the American Revolution,[36] has been reinforced by two more recent developments, one of them intellectual and the other pragmatic.

The former, generated by positivist criminology, consists of the idea of rehabilitation as the major purpose of criminal law: punishment should reeducate the offender. However, the kind and amount of punishment necessary for reeducation differ from one criminal to another. Thus, in three similar cases of murder, the proper sentence may be twenty-five years for one murderer, five years for the other, and just probation (or even discharge) for the third if the third does not constitute risks for the future. Under the impact of this philosophy, American judges have been given sentencing authority within very wide discretionary boundaries. (Similarly, under its impact, indeterminate sentences gave wide discretionary power to parole authorities.)

The second development is pragmatic, consisting of the emergence of plea bargaining—a bureaucratic expediency by whose use 90 percent of criminal dispositions are currently made in America. The expediency further extends discretionary powers. Very often judges, when distributing "negotiated justice," make severity of punishment dependent on bargaining position and skill of the defendant rather than on degree of guilt, and they go as far as either to forgo entirely duly prescribed penalties or to disregard the wide statutory boundaries and impose penalties for crimes different from those committed by the defendant. All this brings about unfortunate effects—the unchecked dispositions are arbitrary, and not only is their injustice wrong per se, but, moreover, it undermines the effectiveness of criminal law.[37]

From this perspective *Furman* constitutes, again, a narrow decision. Discretion in capital cases is but a minute portion of the wide discretionary powers exercised in total criminal dispositions. The underlying notion of the *Furman* ruling is that if a severe punishment is imposed arbitrarily, it is unconstitutional. To be sure, capital punishment is the harshest. However, there are also other severe penalties, all of them often imposed in an arbitrary manner. Consequently, from the *Furman* standpoint, all of them should have been pronounced invalid;[38] but this would require overhauling the criminal justice system—an undertaking out of the province of the Supreme Court.

Furthermore, arbitrariness seems to be less of a threat in infliction of capital punishment than in noncapital cases. It is so, because courts pronounce the death penalty after trial, not in the process of bargaining,[39] and this is, usually, a trial by jury—the jury imposing or at least influencing the punishment. Consequently, the judge is checked and his discretion limited. And, to the degree to which the jury reflects "the conscience of the community" as it is supposed to do, the selection for execution of the few most heinous capital cases should be fairly consistent. Belief in this consistency marked, as late as 1970, the stand of the Court.[40] What *Furman* did was to reverse this stand: not merely judges but also juries have been denounced for arbitrariness and stripped of unstructured discretionary powers in capital cases.[41] Hence, discretion has been banned from the small part of criminal dispositions where it had been least arbitrarily exercised.

CHAPTER 2

FROM FURMAN TO GREGG AND BEYOND

The legal developments to follow *Furman* were as anticipated by Chief Justice Burger in his dissent.[1] To avoid abolition, a large number of the States—altogether thirty-four[2]—as well as the Congress, rushed to pass new statutes. Some of them enacted mandatory death sentences for certain narrowly defined crimes. For instance, the Louisiana statute of 1973 provided that "Whoever commits the crime of the first degree murder shall be punished by death."[3] The majority of the States introduced guidelines specifying conditions under which death sentences might be imposed. For example, according to the Georgia statute, for "an offense which may be punishable by death, a sentence of death should not be imposed unless the jury verdict included a finding of at least one statutory aggravating circumstance and a recommendation that such sentence be imposed."[4] The provision was followed by a catalog of the aggravating circumstances.

The new statutes were quickly challenged in courts. In 1976, in *Gregg v. Georgia*[5] and its companion cases,[6] two questions emerged. First, were death sentences imposed under the new guidelines constitutionally valid? Second, were mandatory death sentences constitutionally valid? When answering, the Court faced three options. It could have answered "no" to both questions in another *Furman*-like repudiation of the newly introduced procedures without finally determining the issue of per se validity of capital punishment. Or it could have accepted total abolition and therefore answered both questions in the negative. Or, finally, it could have answered positively one or both of the questions and thus accepted the per se validity of capital punishment.

This time the Court solved the basic issue by selecting the third option. It invalidated mandatory death sentences,[7] but it sustained the validity of death sentences pronounced (in Georgia, Florida, and Texas) under the new guidelines. In this way the Court rejected total abolition: "We now hold that the punishment of death does not invariably violate the Constitution"— in the words of Justice Stewart.[8]

This decision and these words indicate the extent of the shift in the views of the Court during the four years between *Furman* and *Gregg*. To be sure, Justices Brennan and Marshall did not change their stand; however, they became entirely isolated. The neutral group disappeared: Justice Douglas was replaced by an advocate of capital punishment, and the two other neutrals accepted the retentionist position; thus, they joined the four strict constructionists. In *Furman*, the strict constructionists justified their stand by purely constitutional arguments: separation of powers, federalism, and necessity of judicial restraint. Since *Gregg*, some strict constructionists, as well as the neutrals-turned-retentionists, have gone further: they claim, with varying degree of logical mettle, that capital punishment is morally just or reasonable, or both, and therefore should stay with us; and they use this appraisal to support the antiabolitionist construction.

This is, in particular, the stand accepted, in *Gregg*, by Justices Stewart, Powell, and Stevens. For them, capital punishment became a legitimate expression of the society's moral outrage: "certain crimes are themselves so grievous an affront to humanity that the only adequate response may be the penalty of death."[9] To show that this is not just their personal stand but also the

stand of the society, they refer to the post-*Furman* developments: enactment of new death statutes by thirty-four states is
the "most marked indication of society's endorsement of the
death penalty."[10] They also claim that the many pronouncements of the penalty by juries are another indication by the end
of March 1976, more than 460 persons were sentenced to death
since *Furman*[11] (even though various *Furman* Justices considered comparable pre-*Furman* numbers trivial[12]).

The three Justices add to this a list of teleological arguments.
They quote approvingly Lord Denning, the leading British retentionist: "punishment inflicted for grave crimes should adequately reflect [the society's] revulsion . . . in order to maintain
respect for law."[13] If it does not, they speculate, "the instinct of
retribution [which] is part of the nature of man" will bring about
"the seeds of anarchy—of self-help, vigilante justice, and lynch
law";[14] thus, they assume that in America of today the "mildness"
of genuine life imprisonment for heinous crimes constitutes a
motive for lynching.

The three Justices acknowledge that all the numerous studies
conducted to discover deterrent superiority of capital punishment over imprisonment "have been inconclusive," and "there
is no convincing empirical evidence either supporting or refut-
ing" the claim of the superiority.[15] Nevertheless, they insist (in
nearly the next sentence) that for many crimes other than the
crimes of passion "the death penalty undoubtedly is a significant
deterrent," that is, a deterrent clearly more effective than any
period of confinement.[16] At least some of these contentions are
shared by two other antiabolitionist Justices—White and Rehnquist. They believe that, if not imposed too seldom or arbitrarily,
capital punishment serves "a useful penological function."[17] The
function consists in meeting the widespread need for retribution,[18] in the most secure incapacitation,[19] and in general deterrence. "I . . . need not reject the death penalty as a more
effective deterrent than a lesser punishment," claimed Justice
White already in *Furman*.[20] He repeated this rather circumspect
assertion in *Roberts v. Louisiana*,[21] and, two years later, he

joined Justice Rehnquist in stressing that, when imposed for murder of a police officer, the penalty would be effective "in protecting the foot soldiers of an ordered society."[22] So strong are their convictions that both Justices favor, in this case, a mandatory death penalty;[23] and Justice Rehnquist goes as far as to recommend mandatory capital punishment under the felony-murder rule.[24]

CHAPTER 3

THE MEANING OF
THE LEGAL CHANGE

Where are we now, in the wake of this complex legal development? Following the uncertainties brought about by *Furman*, the law on the books has been largely clarified. The mandatory death penalty, despite the support for it by Justices Rehnquist and White, has been proclaimed, at least basically, unconstitutional.[1] On the other hand, the death penalty is valid when imposed for murder by guided juries or judges, if the guidance is as prescribed by the laws of Georgia, Florida, Texas, and those alike. This prerequisite of guidance in discretion has been called by some Justices a remarkable improvement over earlier practices: "No longer can a jury wantonly and freakishly impose the death sentence; it is always circumscribed by the legislative guidelines."[2] Thus, a new era of justice and consistency of capital dispositions is claimed to have replaced the arbitrariness preceding *Furman*.

This claim is exaggerated; today, the law of capital punishment seems to be almost where it was in the years preceding *Furman*. On the one hand, the mandatory death penalty, nearly unknown before *Furman*,[3] is, again, basically unknown today. On the other hand, the new guidance in discretion did not bring as much difference as its advocates believe, and it could not for the following reasons.

The sentencing process in America is of two varieties: it follows either a trial or a guilty plea, which is most often negotiated. The new guidance in discretion refers only to post-trial sentencing, not to sentencing following a bargain. Whenever plea bargaining occurs, arbitrariness and inconsistency are allowed to prevail. In particular, lightening the sentence within discretionary boundaries does not necessarily result from insignificance of guilt or any other uniform principle but often depends on how all the participants have played the negotiating game. Dismissal of some of the multiple charges is equally arbitrary, and reduction of charge means application of an arbitrarily selected criminal norm that has not been broken at all.[4] In capital cases this arbitrariness means that "some are spared while others are pushed on along the road to execution without any *rule* to govern the choice."[5] Unfortunately, 90 percent of all criminal dispositions in America are settled through plea negotiations; even if the proportion of capital crimes settled in this manner is not that high, it is still preponderant.[6]

Thus, the new guidance in discretion refers only to a small part of dispositions in capital cases; it applies exclusively to post-trial sentencing. However, even there, the impact of the guidance is minor, if any, and the reasons are intrinsic in the post-trial sentencing process. Whenever sentencing follows trial, it is clear what the jurors (or the judge, if he has the sentencing power) are supposed to do. They are supposed to select, within the statutory boundaries, a just punishment. For a punishment to be just, its severity must match the moral sentiment of the society; that is, it must fit the degree of guilt that is experienced by the society in response to the crime committed[7] (or that would be experienced had the society known of the crime). This criterion—the degree of guilt and the ensuing feeling of justice— is an obvious demand in any civilized society, and no alternative may feasibly replace it.

This notion of sentencing does not assume full uniformity of moral evaluations in America; the assumption, unwarranted in any large group, would be evidently false in an open and pluralistic society of today. It assumes, however, a degree of consensus. First, it assumes consensus on what kinds of wrongdoing deserve punishment, that is, on the minimal demands of acceptable behavior that must be enforced. There is, for instance, almost full consensus in the United States that violence against persons, burglary, or arson should be punished, whereas failing to contribute to charities should not. Second, it assumes consensus on relative blameworthiness of those acts that do deserve punishment, and, consequently, on the just severity of punishments. Thus, there seems to be little doubt in America that, all other factors being equal, the more harmful a criminal act to others the more blameworthy it is,[8] and that the intensity of criminal intent does influence the degree of the blame deserved. That is why there is consensus in America that life imprisonment would be unjustly severe for shoplifting or for any involuntary offense and that twenty years is too much for a teenager's joyride.[9] Here, however, one qualification must be made. Wherever a wide consensus on severity of punishments exists, it is rarely a consensus on the precise measure determining exactly how severe a penalty should be. It is rather a feeling that, from some point on, the punishment becomes intolerably severe (or intolerably lenient), as the cited instances of penalties for shoplifting or for a joyride should make clear.

This qualification is of utmost importance for the present considerations; it means that the general moral sentiment constitutes a somewhat vague criterion for the measure of punishment. If a statute provides for robbery a sentencing range from five to ten years, it may be obvious that in the most brutal case, ten, and in its opposite, five years would be fit. However, in the majority of the in-between cases it would be unclear whether seven or eight would do; each penalty may match the dominant feeling of justice. The same holds true with respect to fines: if the fine for an offense ranges from $50 to $100, $70 or $80 may appear equally just in the majority of individual cases. This vagueness unavoidably opens the door to a degree of arbitrariness; even if a jury (or a judge) reflects the moral sentiment of the society as perfectly as it ideally should, the very vagueness of the society's moral sentiment leaves room for vacillation and arbitrary decisions.

There is a paradox to this as old as criminal law itself. One basic prerequisite for justice of criminal dispositions is their consistency—the severity of punishments should be determined by uniform criteria, not arbitrarily; that is, it should be determined in consonance with the fundamental precept *Treat like cases alike, and varying cases according to relevant differences among them.*[10] Sentencing discretion inevitably runs against this precept; it opens the door to a degree of arbitrariness in all the borderline cases where the just measure of punishment is unclear, and such cases constitute the majority of total criminal dispositions. Hence, sentencing discretion brings about injustice.

Paradoxically, however, this very discretion also constitutes a basic prerequisite for justice. In a civilized society, to be just, punishments must fit the amount of guilt, and since for any kind of crime the amount varies from case to case, there must be reasonable room left for discretionary gradation of punitive measures. The room can be provided only by sentencing alternatives and, in particular, sentencing ranges. Without the discretionary gradation, under the system of mandatory sentences, very different cases would be treated, not "according to relevant differences among them," but identically.

There is no perfect solution to this antinomy between injustice of discretion and injustice of lack of discretion. The shape of the necessary compromise depends on the relative seriousness of these two injustices. Civilized societies consider the injustice of lack of discretion grave; sanctioning crimes without room for gradation of guilt is perceived as intolerable today.[11] That is why all modern legal systems provide for discretion in sentencing. The majority of them do so, however, with an important limitation: by avoiding very wide sentencing ranges, they at least keep the penalty-fixing power of the courts within reasonable boundaries.[12]

This compromise is not perfect, of course. When, under the statutory boundaries for confinement for robbery ranging from five to ten years, two robbers whose degree of guilt is indistinguishable meet in prison, one of them convicted for seven and the other for eight years, they rightly experience the sentencing process as running against the precept "treat like cases alike." The same happens to those sentenced to differing fines for an identical offense committed under like conditions. Yet the discrepancy between a somewhat higher and lower fine, and even between a somewhat longer or shorter period of confinement, however disappointing, is relatively narrow. It thus constitutes an apparently tolerable price for preservation of the sentencing discretion.

Not so if the discretion amounts to choice between imprisonment and execution: the discrepancy turns from narrow to immense. Therefore, if in two cases of a capital crime where the degree of guilt is indistinguishable, one defendant is sent to confinement and the other to the gallows, the arbitrariness becomes hardly tolerable. This arbitrariness is unavoidable, however, in all those borderline cases of any capital crime where, owing to the vagueness of the dominant moral sentiment, life imprisonment and death penalty are both experienced as more or less equally justified.

Unfortunately, the majority of capital crimes constitute such borderline cases. To be sure, sometimes capital cases occur where, in a manner evident to all, the degree of guilt is, even for a capital crime, enormous or where the degree is exceptionally low. Manson may be an instance of the former. Sandra Lockett, who owing to the oddity of felony-murder rule became a murderer without killing or willing to kill,[13] is an instance of the latter. However, the majority of capital cases are on the vague border; to make this clear, it is enough to look even at the murder cases already discussed, for instance at *Gregg v. Georgia* and three of its companion cases—*Proffitt v. Florida, Jurek v. Texas*, and *Roberts v. Louisiana*. Roberts fired, in the course of an armed robbery, four shots into the head of a gas station attendant, an old man who had already been over-powered.[14] Proffitt stabbed and killed his victim when burglar-izing his home at dawn and beat the victim's wife.[15] Gregg, when hitchhiking with a companion, was picked up by two men. He then ordered the two men to come up an embankment and shot them; when they fell down he shot again, at close range, into the head of each, took their valuables, and drove away.[16] Jurek kidnapped a 10-year-old girl, attempted to rape her, choked her, and threw her unconscious body into the river, where she drowned.[17] From the standpoint of justice, where is the de-marcation between the cases where life imprisonment is clearly proper and those that exclusively demand the death penalty? Was Roberts' murder cruel enough to make life imprisonment too lenient? If not, was Proffitt's butchery? If, again not, was the fact of two killings by Gregg? Or attempted rape and accom-plished murder of a child? Even if one adds various details to each of these cases, no clear demarcation line may be drawn: in each of them genuine life imprisonment would be widely per-ceived as fairly just, and so would the penalty of death. This vagueness of the society's feeling of guilt and of justice makes a degree of arbitrariness unavoidable in capital cases, and no statutory guidance in discretion can feasibly change this. That is why the new statutory guidelines appear to be a hopeless at-tempt to do the impossible[18] or to be just window dressing by lawmakers to mollify the Court.

And, indeed, they seem to be not much more than window dressing. More than that, since *Gregg*, the Court, having ac-cepted the window dressing, did itself forgo the infeasible ideal of full consistency of capital dispositions. Thus, under the new statute of Georgia, "[a] person convicted of murder shall be pun-ished by death or by imprisonment for life";[19] and, to make the choice, "the judge shall consider, or shall include in his instruc-tions to the jury for it to consider, any mitigating circumstances or aggravating circumstances."[20] This is only the traditional idea, however expressed in a somewhat new wording: the judge or jury should measure (through the consideration of the mitigating and aggravating circumstances) the degree of guilt and use it as criterion for a just selection of the death sentence or confinement. To be sure, a list of aggravating circumstances has been added to this general formula by Georgia lawmakers, and the death penalty may not be imposed unless at least one of the listed items did occur. However, the list consists not only in a long catalog of whatever obviously makes murder particularly blameworthy; it also includes one very broad item—that the offense "was outrageously or wantonly vile, horrible or inhuman in that it involved torture, depravity of mind, or an aggravated battery to the victim."[21] What all this clearly amounts to is making, behind the screen of the wordy new provisions, the death sentence simply contingent upon the degree of guilt and feeling of justice, and this means a return to the stand preceding *Furman* by both the law of Georgia and by the Court, which approved this law in *Gregg*.

The same holds true for the new laws of Florida and Texas. In Florida, where murder is punished by life imprisonment or death, the statute lists a large number of rather obvious aggravating and mitigating circumstances, each of them indicating the degree of guilt; one aggravating circumstance is that the crime "was especially heinous, atrocious or cruel."[22] The court, helped by nonbinding advice of the jury, "shall enter a sentence of life imprisonment or death . . . . after weighing the aggravating and mitigating circumstances."[23]

Texas law seems, on its face, to be more restrictive, especially on the mitigating circumstances. Still, in its functioning, it is like the laws of Georgia and Florida. In particular, one prerequisite for imposition of the death sentence for capital murder is that the jury find unanimously and "beyond reasonable doubt" that "there is a probability that the defendant would commit criminal acts of violence that would constitute a continuing threat to society."[24] Under this odd formula,[25] as interpreted by Texas courts, the jury may and should consider all kinds of mitigating circumstances, and this interpretation has been approved, in *Jurek*, by the Supreme Court of the United States.[26]

In another 1976 decision, dealing with the new law of North Carolina, the Court demanded that, in capital cases, "the character and record of the individual offender and the circumstances of the particular offense" be considered;[27] two years later, the Court made a claim that the sentencer "not be precluded from considering, *as a mitigating factor*, any aspect of a defendant's character or record and any of the circumstances of the offense that the defendant proffers as a basis for a sentence less than death," since "an individualized decision is essential in capital cases."[28] Thus, here again, nothing specific, but the degree of guilt and feeling of justice are the final criteria for the life or death determination.

In this manner, after the suspense following 1972, the pendulum swung back, and we returned where we had been in the days preceding *Furman*. The return is not full, to be sure; a few changes did occur. First, many states have accepted a bifurcated proceeding—a separate sentencing hearing with relaxed evidence rules that may provide additional, relevant information. The design, favored by the Court but not deemed essential in capital cases,[29] is not new: "This is the analogue of the procedure in the ordinary case when capital punishment is not in issue; the court conducts a separate inquiry before imposing sentence."[30] Another change, aimed at increased consistency of dispositions, is an automatic review of all death sentences.[31] If properly implemented,[32] the review may be of utmost importance in the few extreme cases, especially when the insignificance of guilt in a capital crime demands leniency and, because of error, bias, or abuse, death sentence has been pronounced.[33]

On the other hand, irrespective of whether death or incarceration has been pronounced, review of the sentence, automatic or not, is of somewhat minor value in all the borderline cases of capital crimes where both confinement and death penalty are experienced as equally justified. (One more change implemented exclusively by the Court, and not by lawmakers, consists in a limitation of the list of capital crimes. In *Coker v. Georgia*, the Court pronounced the death sentence a cruel punishment for rape of an adult woman where no life was lost.[34] This new ban on a penalty too harsh for the crime committed is, however, an extension of the *Weems* decision[35] and has nothing to do with discretion and arbitrariness in deciding capital cases.)

The insignificance of these few changes, and the basic return to the pre-*Furman* practice, found some corroboration in the bit of empirical data at hand[36] and were stressed with particular bluntness by Justice White in *Lockett v. Ohio*: "The Court has now completed its about-face since *Furman v. Georgia. . . . Furman* held that as a result of permitting the sentencer to exercise unfettered discretion . . . , any given death sentence was cruel and unusual. . . . Today the Court holds again . . . that the sentencer may constitutionally impose the death penalty only as an exercise of his unguided discretion.[37]

All this constitutes an odd development of legal doctrine. Having overcome, in *Furman*, dissent of the strict constructionists, the Court did, in fact, invalidate the majority of state capital laws and some federal norms as well. The retentionist lawmakers were forced to enact new capital statutes. However, *Furman* constituted an ambiguous ruling. It demanded "an undetermined measure of change from the various state lawmakers and the Congress."[38] In particular, it did not make clear whether discretion should be totally eliminated or only limited. Consequently, while some states were experimenting with guided discretion, others introduced mandatory death sentences and thus provoked new invalidations. In response to the new invalidations, another legislative effort was made—the lawmakers rushed to replace mandatory sentences by guided discretion. Eventually, all this resulted almost in a return to the pre-*Furman* system, and the Court approved the return, as if it were saying about its own stand in *Furman*: we did not really mean it.

It would be difficult to overestimate the costs of this about-face. Obviously, they include efforts and expenditure, especially on the part of the states, inherent in the very fact of the recurring legal changes, and, since eventually the efforts and expenditure did not produce any significant change, they have been carried out nearly for naught. This engagement of the states by the Court in an almost empty exercise engenders a degree of constitutional strain. More importantly the about-face runs against some basic values underlying our legal system. One of them is the long-term predictability of the legal response to human behavior and the resulting predictability of human behavior itself. The predictability disappears when important legal norms change very often and even more so when their meaning becomes clouded in the process of the frequent change. Another value compromised is the moral influence of law. It is one of the law's, and especially of the Supreme Court's, functions to help shape the general moral sentiment, and on an issue of such moral weight as the death penalty, the function has hardly been performed at all by the deeply divided, vague, and oscillating Court. It is also dubious whether *Furman* and the subsequent decisions did anything to enhance the Court's and the law's prestige.

What is the explanation for this rather unfortunate development of the legal doctrine? Why did the Court take part in it? What can we expect from the future? In particular, will capital punishment be abolished or stay with us indefinitely? These questions will be dealt with in the following chapters. One of the conclusions will be that the Court is not to blame. The legal development under discussion has been produced by a unique clash of conflicting social forces with none of them under the Court's control. One of the forces is a general tendency of social evolution toward decreasing severity of criminal punishments. The other one is the shifting sentiment in America during the last fifteen years from leniency to severity in dealing with offenders. The shift has been generated by the spreading anger about crime and fear of crime, and the anger and fear result from the decay of the criminal justice system. The following analysis of these forces will not only provide an explanation for the odd development of law but will also make feasible a cautious prediction on the future of the death penalty in America.

PART TWO

THE EVOLUTION

CHAPTER 4

SOCIAL EVOLUTION AND CRIMINAL PUNISHMENT

SOME GENERAL REMARKS

The spread of the abolitionist sentiment preceding *Furman* was not a uniquely American event. It was a display of a general regularity—social evolution brings a tendency toward decreasing severity of criminal punishments. The tendency, having operated in America, provides an explanation for the abolitionist stand of some Justices and for the hesitant stand of others. This is a vague explanation, however, which must be specified: there are few notions as ambiguous as that of social evolution.

The notion is not universally accepted.[1] Among those who accept it and claim the occurrence of the evolution, there is general consensus on one semantic issue: they understand by "social evolution" a directional social change. Here, however, the agreement ends, and everything else is contested. In particular, the evolutionary thinkers dispute what it is that evolves, which forces produce the evolution, and what the direction of the evolutionary sequence is.

What is it that evolves? According to one view, individual societies change independently of one another and in varying directions. This is so since the evolution of each society is predetermined by such factors as the society's specific environment, its distinct cultural heritage, and peculiarities of its elite. In the view of others, individual societies change independently of one another, but they go through similar steps in the same direction owing to some universal regularities of social development. Still others claim that the evolution of particular societies, however it goes, adds up to an overall evolution of human society as a whole.

The mainsprings of the evolution are also controversial. Proponents of historicist doctrines claim to have detected various forces that, according to laws of science, inevitably predetermine the exact direction of the social change. Others speak, more cautiously, about conditionally operating forces that produce developmental tendencies rather than an inevitable course of human history. Whatever their operation, conditional or not, it is unclear what these forces consist of—advocates of various evolutionary theories are here, again, in disagreement. Many of them profess economism—new technology brings about economic change that subsequently changes all other components of the social structure.[2] Rationalists and idealists offer a list of opposite explanations—it is human reason that causes the society to evolve in the view of Condorcet, or morality and law according to Petrażycki, or the mystical, self-creating force of Hegelian ideas. Social Darwinists construct a social analogue to natural selection—the human race evolves through elimination of the weak in the struggle for survival among individuals, groups, and nations.

Another analogue has been offered by a variety of functional analysts. They treat any society as if it were a living, growing, and increasingly complex organism. Thus, the society must fight for survival (whatever "survival" of a society may mean) against its natural environment, surrounding groups, and problems of its own growth. In this struggle the social evolution means the society's improving adaptive capacity. The forces producing the thus understood evolutionary process are, again, identified by use of still another analogy to natural selection: in any society, a tendency to eliminate dysfunctional components of social behavior and to select "those features of a culture which are more suited to maintaining the community,"[3] apparently exists.[4]

This variety of views makes it clear that the direction of the evolutionary change has been contested as well. The directions most often claimed include increasing complexity of the society, its growing adaptability, or achievement of some specific outcome, such as political freedom, classlessness, or benevolence. Some of these claims do not imply any evaluation of where the movement goes; for instance, there apparently is nothing superior in greater complexity. Others explicitly stress the superiority of the ongoing change and thus identify evolution with progress. Still others, for example, some Social Darwinist ideas, are expressed as if they were merely objective propositions, but evaluations are there, and they are barely hidden.

Amidst this confusion, what is the meaning of the claim that social evolution brings a tendency toward decreasing severity of criminal punishments? When claiming this, I am using the expression "social evolution" in a sense that, however relevant to some of the just enumerated notions, is identical with none. In particular, I am not endorsing any of the just mentioned broad evolutionary ideas (even though some of them may contain most promising cues for the future development of knowledge). I am accepting here only a stipulative definition, that is, a definition that selects one specific kind of directional social change and designates it as social evolution. The kind selected here is reasonably clear (or, at least, less vague than many others), rather simple, and fruitful for this book. It consists in the society's becoming more civilized, as indicated by three simultaneous developments that, indeed, most often go together. First, the society experiences increase and increasing spread of knowledge—both scientific and technical. Second, there is development of arts and their spreading appreciation, which increasingly influence aesthetics of human behavior. Third, and most importantly for these considerations, the population becomes more socialized. This means that it increasingly avoids socially harmful behavior, especially aggressive, destructive, or corrupt activities; members of the group perform with increasing effectiveness what is socially useful—they work better, fulfill stipulated obligations, and meet a rising variety of other social commitments; and this growing solidarity expands—it first operates within a small social group, such as a tribe or a city-state, then within a larger geographic area or a nation, and then, following development of trade, transportation, and spread of ideas, it sometimes tends to embrace all of the civilized world or even all of the human race. Thus understood, social evolution may also be called, and is called in the comments to follow, "cultural progress," since all these developments are so widely perceived as valuable that their conjunction comes close to what many of us understand as progress in ordinary language.

It is obvious that these three developments, each of them in a way psychological, imply more than their wording explicitly conveys. Many social changes are necessary to produce these developments; and, once the developments go on, many further social changes follow. Usually, these changes include economic growth that is both conducive to the cultural progress thus understood and, in feedback, is itself stimulated by the progress. The changes also usually include urban growth and increasing division of labor and complexity of the social system. They include the rise, and rising influence, of various elites, especially intellectual, technical, and artistic. They may include the political transition from despotism to democracy—again, the social evolution in this understanding is conducive to the transition, and the transition itself further stimulates the evolution. Thus, there are many broader socioeconomic implications of the society's becoming increasingly civilized. A comprehensive analysis of these implications is unnecessary for this book, but some of them will be touched on soon.

It is the social evolution in this sense that brings about a tendency toward decreasing severity of criminal punishments. The tendency itself is fairly simple: the same kind of criminal behavior tends to be punished less severely on a higher level of social development. This decrease in severity materializes in a variety of ways. For instance, mandatory death penalties for various crimes in Draconian Athens were replaced, from Solon on, by the death penalty's depending on the jury's discretion. Or, whereas in early Rome all homicides had been capital, after the enactment of the XII Tables, unintentional homicide was punished by a minor religious sacrifice only. Or pickpockets were multilated to death in England until the early sixteenth century, tortured less elaborately and killed during the following 300 years, and then confined, often for life, in chains, in the prison hulks; today they face penalties from probation to a few years under comparatively humane conditions. From this a clear corollary follows: the few harshest penalties known to a society tend to disappear once the society reaches a higher level of evolution.[5]

This understanding of the tendency toward decreasing severity of penalties does not imply prophecies; in particular, it does not mean that social evolution leads eventually to the total disappearance of criminal sanctions.[6] Nor does it imply that social evolution brings about decline of the number of acts defined as criminal. To be sure, it causes disappearance of some; social evolution consists, in particular, in society's becoming more knowledgeable, and therefore it leads to removal from the catalogue of crimes those acts that, like heresy or witchcraft, had been included owing to ignorance. On the other hand, growing economy and social complexity and the ever-emerging new problems and new social demands tend to extend crime catalogues while social progress goes on. Therefore the catalogues of many modern societies are longer than those of their less civilized predecessors, who knew nothing about corporate crime, eavesdropping, aircraft piracy, or violating election laws.[7]

The regularity I am discussing here does not imply accepting any of the broad evolutionary and especially historicist doctrines mentioned before. It is just a conditional assertion: whenever cultural progress occurs, the tendency toward decreasing severity of criminal punishments follows. The assertion does not claim anything more. In particular, it does not claim that the progress thus understood must occur or does occur in all or in the majority of human societies. Indeed, a look into history and anthropology suggests that the opposite may be true. Only a limited number of societies in the past has gone through significant periods of progress. In particular, the progress occurred in some ancient societies, and, then, in modern times, in various European nations. On the other hand, the majority of the primitive societies of the past never did enter longer periods of the evolutionary sequence, and some of those that did have reached a high level of civilized life only to decline subsequently. Thus, the conditional assertion proposed here is modest; it refers to periods of progress discernible in a limited number of societies.

Historical evidence implies that this modest assertion is true. The evidence comes from both the ancient world and the history of modern, especially European, civilized societies. To be sure, the paucity of the ancient data and the wealth of the European data make the modern evidence more nearly complete. Despite its flaws, however, our knowledge of at least two most developed ancient societies—Athens and Rome—has corroborative value.

ATHENS

Since the rise, after great migrations, of the city-states all over Greece, through Solon's reforms, to the era of democracy and enlightenment in Athens in the fifth and fourth centuries, B.C., the growth of Greek, and especially Athenian civilization has become a genuine triumph on all three counts mentioned earlier. First, Greek philosophy and Greek arts flourished—the former originally in Ionia, in the seventh and sixth centuries B.C., then in Italian colonies, and, from the fifth century B.C., foremost in Athens. In particular, mathematics, physics, and astronomy thrived, from the Ionians on. There were important developments in psychology from Empedocles to Aristotle. With Herodotus and Thucydides the science of history was born, and zoology and botany were born with Aristotle. Epistemology was cultivated in a variety of ways, especially by Democritus, Socrates, Plato, and Aristotle, and so were moral and political theory (even though sometimes hardly distinguishable from normative morality and political recommendations). And in the fine arts, since the earliest days interwoven with religion, the Greeks reached mastery in Periclean Athens.

All these achievements had a widespread impact on the society. The Athenians, a remarkably curious and vigorous people, were, in the marketplace and around, involved in intellectual debate, and the debate often engaged the philosophers—familiar figures in the town of up to 200,000 citizens.[8] Also, the influence of fine arts has always been remarkable. From the sixth century B.C. onward, Athenian boys read the *Iliad* and the *Odyssey* and learned music and singing.[9] The fifth century brought maturation of drama—at Dionysian festivals Athenians were moved by the tragedies of Aeschylus and Sophocles and enjoyed Aristophanic comedy. They were daily exposed to the treasures of sculpture and architecture on the Acropolis. And the wealthy increasingly possessed masterpieces of ceramic arts at home.

Not unrelatedly, the progress in socialization was imposing. Historically and geographically, barbarian cruelties were not that distant: it was in Miletus during Thales' time when, in the course of an acute class struggle, "the people were at first victorious and murdered the wives and children of the aristocrats; then the aristocrats prevailed and burned their opponents alive, lighting up the open spaces of the city with live torches."[10] In Periclean Athens, there were major flaws in the social system, especially slavery and limitation of the rights of women. Nonetheless, cruelties of the earlier days were gone, everyday life was well ordered, and manners were friendly. The Athenian citizen learned to respond to the growing demands of society. He learned to work efficiently in an expanding and increasingly diversified industrial production, in intensive cultivation of vineyards and olive groves, and in marine trade with the colonies of the Greek empire and various parts of the barbarian world. He learned to widen education of the youth (which was compulsory in classical Athens) and to transfer some of his income for various public services. Most conspicuously he learned to participate in the political process of the democratic state. His social maturity was reflected well—even if in a somewhat idealized manner—in the famous oration of Pericles at the funeral of the war dead:

When a citizen distinguishes himself, then he will be called to serve the state, in preference to others, not as a matter of privilege, but as a reward of merit; and poverty is no bar. . . . The freedom we enjoy extends also to ordinary life; we are not suspicious of one another, and do not nag our neighbour if he chooses to go his own way. . . . But this freedom does not make us lawless. We are taught to respect the magistrates and the laws, and never to forget that we must protect the injured. And we are also taught to observe those unwritten laws whose sanction lies only in the universal feeling of what is right. . . .

Our city is thrown open to the world; we never expel a foreigner. . . . We are free to live exactly as we please, and yet we are always ready to face any danger. . . . We love beauty without indulging in fancies, and although we try to improve our intellect, this does not weaken our will. . . . To admit one's poverty is no disgrace with us; but we consider it disgraceful not to make an effort to avoid it. An Athenian citizen does not neglect public affairs when attending to his private business. . . . We consider a man who takes no interest in the state not as harmless, but as useless; and *although only a few may originate a policy, we are all able to judge it.* We do not look upon discussion as a stumbling-block in the way of political action, but as an indispensable preliminary to acting wisely. . . . We believe that happiness is the fruit of freedom and freedom that of valor, and we do not shrink form the dangers of war. . . . To sum up, I claim that Athens is the School of Hellas, and that the individual Athenian grows up to develop a happy versatility, a readiness for emergencies, and self-reliance.[11]

How did criminal law respond to this growth of culture? Emerging gradually from blood feud and composition of the Homeric age,[12] it was originally a very harsh law—both in the period preceding the enactment of Draco's code and under Draco (who rewrote a mass of existing customary law).[13] To be sure, Draco's code was more humane than the previous norms. It at least helped to prevent the archons and the Areopagus from imposing arbitrary penalties.[14] Moreover, it brought about a clear distinction between intentional and unintentional homicide; the former was punished by death and the latter more leniently—a distinction unknown or blurred earlier; thus, the code proclaimed, "probably for the first time in the ancient world, the importance in law of the doctrine of moral responsibility."[15] Disclaimers notwithstanding,[16] belief in the proverbial harshness of the Draconian code seems to be warranted by those scanty sources that are available,[17] and especially by Plutarch's claim:

[O]ne penalty was assigned to almost all transgressions, namely death, so that even those convicted of idleness were put to death, and those who stole salad or fruit received the same punishment as those who committed sacrilege or murder. Therefore Demades, in later times, made a hit when he said that Draco's laws were written not with ink but blood. And Draco himself, they say, being asked why he made death the penalty for most offenses, replied that in his opinion the lesser ones deserved it, and for the greater ones no heavier penalty could be found.[18]

In the light of both history and anthropology, this great harshness of penalties seems to be a universal characteristic of all criminal laws that newly emerge in early civilizations. This was the case with the laws of the other ancient peoples whose legal history is known to us, such as the Sumerian codes, the laws of Eshunna, the codes of Hammurabi and of the Middle Assyria, the code of Li K'nei in China, and that of Manu in India. Extreme harshness pervaded medieval laws all over Europe—an issue to which I return later. And the more recent primitive peoples have displayed a similar degree of severity once their criminal laws emerged, among them various Indian tribes in the Americas, and African, especially West African, societies.[19]

Thus, Draco seems to have prescribed the mandatory death penalty for almost any crime. What the list of the crimes was we do not know; we know hardly anything specific about Draco's code except for the norms on homicide.[20] According to Plutarch, the list included idleness and theft—even petty larceny. It must also have included various acts against political powerholders—especially Areopagus and archons, treason, military and religious crimes, robbery, arson, mayhem, sexual offenses, and a number of other crimes characteristic of societies on a similar level of development.[21]

As indicated earlier, Draco himself brought about some alleviation of the preceding harshness, at least by removing unintentional acts from the list of capital crimes. A further alleviation came in 594–93 B.C.; Solon, in the words of Plutarch, "repealed the laws of Draco, all except those concerning homicide, because they were too severe and their penalties too heavy."[22] During more than two centuries following Solon, the severity seems to have further declined.

To be sure, this decline does not imply abolition of the death penalty. Not only did the list of capital crimes continue to be substantial, but also some new items were added to it in response to new or increasingly annoying problems or to new demands of the developing society. For instance, procuring a free woman for seduction had been fined by Solon's law, but in the fourth century it was a capital offense, and misleading the people— especially through false promises to the Ekklesia—emerged as a capital crime following establishment of democracy.[23]

Nonetheless, the death penalty became restricted to the wrongs perceived by the increasingly civilized Athenians as most serious. In particular, we know that the penalty disappeared as a sanction for idleness,[24] all but the most aggravated kinds of theft,[25] and destruction of sacred olive trees,[26] and it was no more a sanction for the majority of the acts that, we can safely assume, had been capital crimes under Draco's code. Moreover, from Solon on, the mandatory death penalty was limited to a small and further declining number of gravest felonies such as temple robbery, high treason,[27] or intentional homicide.[28] With respect to the majority of capital crimes, it was left to the jury's discretion whether to impose death or a milder punishment. Another kind of discretion limiting the amount of executions (and of some other penalties as well) was exercised by the Ekklesia through amnesties and the pardoning power. Thus, the application of the most severe penalty was on the decline. The manner of its application was also evolving: there was at least some, however incongruous, shifting to more humane ways of execution, from hurling the convict alive into a pit (which superseded ancient stoning) and the cruelty of *tympanon* to poisoning by a drink of hemlock.[29]

This decline in severity was not limited to capital punishment. Some other very harsh sanctions tended either to disappear as the response to a specific kind of offense or to totally disappear. Thus, for bribery, the outlawry—a sanction amounting to expulsion from Attica—was replaced, in the fourth century B.C., by a fine.[30] Two other punishments (neither of them, however, purely criminal) disappeared. They were, first, selling an Athenian citizen to slavery, and, second, his direct enslavement. The former, a sanction imposed on girls for fornication, did apparently fade through desuetude.[31] The latter, a sanction for insolvent debtors, was repealed by Solon. It was replaced by civil remedies for private debts and, for public debts, by multiplication of the debt, disfranchisement until the debt was paid, and sometimes imprisonment; the threat of imprisonment was becoming increasingly milder during the fifth and fourth centuries.[32]

All these developments seem to corroborate the claim that cultural progress results in the decline of punitive harshness. However, because of scantiness of sources, this is a somewhat rough corroboration; the shortage of data makes us unable to clearly trace the many specific steps through which the criminal law of Athens must have gone. About one hundred speeches of the Attic orators delivered at courts in the late fifth and the fourth centuries are the main source of our knowledge, as well as scattered remarks by philosophers, historians, and dramatic poets. These sources provide us with some information about criminal punishments in the last period of Athenian independence. But we can learn very little from them about the development of penalties during the two preceding centuries of cultural progress; we are unclear even about criminal punishments enacted by Solon himself despite all our insights into his economic, political, and procedural reforms. To be sure, the fourth century orators refer to the law of their own day, especially criminal law, as the "laws of Solon." No clear evidence about the text of Solon's norms on punishments was available to them, however, and they often make these references "even when there is actually no doubt that [a norm] does not go back to Solon's time."[33] Clearly, their references to the great figure of the past were often used "to strengthen their arguments by endowing with a mystical sanctity whatever law they were relying on at the moment, provided its origin was not sufficiently recent to be present to the minds of the audience."[34]

ROME

After the battle of Chaeronea in 338 B.C., Athens as well as the rest of Greece, fell under the Macedonian rule, and the following centuries brought about a gradual decline of Greek civilization. When Greek city-states were losing their independence, an opposite process was going on in Italy, where a new empire was in formation.

Rome emerged in or around the eighth century B.C. The original monarchy was replaced about 508 by an aristocratic republic, and then, after almost five centuries of wars, expansion, and internal strife, by an autocracy. Since the establishment of the Republic, Rome had grown from a tribal city-state to the master of Italy and the Western Mediterranean in the third century B.C. to an empire nearly identical with the civilized world. Its remarkable political growth was uneven and stormy and suffered from setbacks. And so was the growth of its civilization, which paradoxically reached its peak under Augustus after the destruction of the republican rule.

This was a civilization largely borrowed from the Greeks. The Romans never produced any original philosophical system—they adopted the ideas of various Greek schools. Also in some technical fields, progress was beholden to Greek knowledge. The most important areas in which the Romans appeared original and creative were such applied disciplines as engineering, administrative science, and, in particular, jurisprudence, which in the course of its spectacular growth from the republican *veteres* to the great jurists of the Principate stimulated the brilliant development of civil law.

The dependence on the Greeks was even stronger in fine arts; just as the Greek gods were adopted under Latin names by the Romans, so was the style of the gods' statues and temples. Stimulated by the Greek genius, the Romans eventually developed the great, imperial architecture of Augustus and the Flavians. They also had remarkable literary achievements—their poetry came of age in the last century of the Republic, and it flourished in Augustus' days.

The progress in socialization was uneven and often marred by wars and class friction. From its emergence to the Principate, Rome was continually immersed in major wars, originally defensive, and since the last Punic war deliberately imperial. Their frequency and intensity stimulated the growth of a professional army that became an increasingly hard-to-check political force. The struggle of the poor against the rich pervaded the history of the Republic in a variety of ways to culminate in the Gracchi revolution. The following civil wars, which began in 88 B.C., made the army the ultimate powerbroker and resulted in establishment of military autocracy. The wars and class strife had a demoralizing impact in various periods of Roman history—on the small-holders' losing their land to wealthy landlords in the wake of Punic wars; on the senatorial class, made largely corrupt by the wars of the late Republic; and on the legionnaires, who were fighting for pay, booty, and land to be seized from previous holders. Furthermore, the ruthlessness of civil war had a general debasing influence.

Despite these setbacks, the progress in socialization was, on the whole, remarkable. In the early Republic, social solidarity was narrowly limited; to whatever degree solidarity implied "do not harm your neighbor," the neighbors not to be harmed were inhabitants of the city-state of Rome, not members of the surrounding tribes, with which Rome had been in a nearly permanent state of war. The following centuries brought about an ever-growing spread of solidarity. To be sure, this spread was at first hampered by wars. However, the conquests following the wars produced, through a series of territorial acquisitions, establishment of the worldwide empire, which paved the way to the new solidarity of the civilized man.

The solidarity reached its apogee under the Principate. *Pax Romana*, as implemented by Augustus, meant worldwide spread of peace, security, and order for all under an effective administration. The peace prompted diffusion of Graeco-Roman culture, and a similar, urban way of socioeconomic life was spreading all over the empire. This emerging unity found an important expression in Stoic ideas of human brotherhood and equality—the ideas that gained a new influence in Rome. Under the impact of these conditions, the body of Roman citizens was constantly expanding; the extension of citizenship to the whole of Italy had been accomplished before the end of the Republic, and admission to Roman franchise continued, by stages, under the Principate. Moreover, the operation of *ius gentium* was drawing the condition of the aliens closer to that of Roman citizens. Thus, the principle "do not harm your neighbor" acquired a new, universal sense.

This growing proportion of citizens and near-citizens became ever better trained in socially useful behavior of increasing variety, much of it economic. The economic growth of Rome was uneven and troubled, especially in agriculture. Nevertheless, the growth was marked, stimulated by the territorial expansion of the state. The expansion eventually produced a worldwide market; diffusion of agricultural, industrial, and commercial skills; and accumulation of capital, especially in the city of Rome. Under the Principate, the city became the main financial center of the world. All this provided widespread training in various skills and, most importantly, in the motivation to work and to fulfill economic commitments. The training was reinforced by the ingeniously developed provisions of civil law, in particular

the norms of contracts, quasi-contracts, and torts. The socializing impact of these norms—with their stress on fulfillment of
obligations, rectification of wrongdoing, good faith, decency of
commercial habits, and clean hands as a prerequisite for access
to courts of justice—can hardly be overstated.[35]

The training in the socially useful behavior was not limited to
economic activities. The Roman republic never became a democracy, but from its establishment through the third century
B.C., it was steadily democratized owing to plebeian victories.
This implied the growing social involvement of an increasing
body of citizens, which, in the capital, largely survived the end
of the republic. This involvement had also been marked in the
provinces, where colonies and towns traditionally enjoyed broad
self-government. Their autonomy was strengthened under the
Principate when Augustus imposed new checks on provincial
governors; thus, provincial towns were nearly free from central
control, at least in nonfiscal matters. They were administered
by elective councils and elective magistrates who, following the
example of the capital, provided sanitation, gardens, temples,
theaters, libraries, education, free food supplies, and free en-
tertainment for the poor. In this way, under the reign of Augustus—the era of the highest development of Roman civilization—Italy and the provinces became a federation of
autonomous towns and their territories, each town being "an
association of men with common habits and needs and interests
. . . who endeavor by united effort to create for themselves acceptable and convenient surroundings for life."[36]

The XII Tables, promulgated in the middle of the fifth century
B.C., reflect largely the archaic customary law of the period preceding their enactment. In the fifth century, the republic was
already organized well enough to restrain primitive self-help as
response to wrongdoing but not to eliminate it—the state was
unable to prosecute and sanction by itself all kinds of socially
harmful behavior. Thus, there emerged two kinds of punishments for wrongdoing—one of them implemented in a suit at

public law and the other delictual. The former involved not only public proceedings but also public prosecution and public execution of punishment. The latter originated at the plaintiff's request and in this early period it was the plaintiff's business to carry out the authorized execution.

What offenses belonged, under XII Tables, to which group, is not easy to say—the surviving fragments of the Tables come to us second hand, from not always reliable sources. The "public" crimes apparently included treason, embezzlement of public funds, false witness, and the removal of crops by magic. The classification of acts such as murder, arson, corruption by a judge, or cutting a neighbor's crops by night is unclear.[37] Nonpayment of a debt is a "private" crime, as well as theft, various kinds of damage to property, assault, and some insults. (Oddly enough, such acts as theft and assault remained delictual through the classical period of the Roman law; thus, in Rome, they were always punished through the civil action of the injured party.) Despite the difference in the procedure, norms sanctioning both groups of acts played a similar function: they were used for punishment of wrongdoing (and not just for restitution), and that is why they should all be treated as norms of criminal law. In Mommsen's words, "the fundamental characteristic of the broken moral law and the following reprisal provided by the state unites both fields thoroughly and thus the distinction between the enforcement in public or private proceedings appears insignificant and incidental."[38]

The reprisals of the XII Tables were severe, with the death penalty as the most common sanction; the other, milder penalties included talion for serious physical injuries.[39] Those guilty of treason were beheaded, and false witnesses were flung from the Tarpeian rock.[40] Corruption by a judge[41] and bribery at elections[42] were capital offenses, as well as, apparently, various kinds of witchcraft—evil incantations, use of charms to draw a neighbor's crops, and enticement from a neighbor's land of the powers that cause seeds to grow.[43] Intentional homicide was a capital crime as well—the existing sources imply that the culprit was scourged and drowned.[44] A thief caught in the act, if he was a free man, was scourged and adjudicated into the victim's power, and it seems that the victim might then kill the thief, sell him into slavery abroad, or accept ransom.[45] If a thief was a slave, he was scourged and thrown from the Tarpeian rock.[46] A thief caught at night might be lawfully killed on the spot.[47] For the theft of crops at night by an adult, the penalty was crucifixion,[48] and for arson, scourging and then being burned alive.[49] Peculation and sacrilege—theft of state property and religious property, respectively—were punished by death (however, it is unclear whether the sanction was imposed by XII Tables or another ancient law).[50] And an insolvent debtor was handed over to his creditor, who could kill him or sell him into slavery abroad; if there were several creditors, they could cut the debtor's body into pieces corresponding to the amount of their respective claims.[51]

The centuries following enactment of the XII Tables brought about an increasing decline in this harshness. Indeed, even the law of the XII Tables itself was, in some respects, more lenient and humane than the preceding customary norms. In particular, it limited the arbitrary judicial powers of patrician magistrates. It also made various punishments dependent on the degree of guilt in a way similar to Draco's and Solon's laws (and probably under their influence).[52] Thus, whereas intentional homicide and arson were capital crimes, unintentional killing was sanctioned by the duty to offer a ram,[53] and unintentional fire setting, by paying damages or, if the culprit was too poor to pay, by light spanking.[54] Likewise, while an adult was crucified for having stolen crops at night, a minor was punished by scourging or paying damages.[55] Another limitation on primitive harshness may have preceded enactment of the XII Tables. According to tradition, a Roman citizen convicted in Rome, by a magistrate, to death or fine above a certain limit was given, by *Lex Valeria* of 509 B.C., a right to *provocatio*, that is, to an appeal to the people against the sentence.[56]

In the period between the XII Tables and the beginnings of

the Principate, the harshness of penalties gradually subsided. In particular, the imposition of the death penalty was on the decline through both legislation and court practice. Thus, the death penalty for insolvent debtors had already been abolished in the fourth century.[57] Sometime later, the execution of a common thief caught in the act disappeared, and the victim maintained only a civil action for a multiple value of the stolen property;[58] this change encompassed thieves of crops at night (whose crucifixion had disappeared much earlier).[59] Removal of common theft from the list of capital crimes was followed by the removal of peculation and sacrilege.[60] The originally capital crime of electoral bribery was met, in the late Republic and early Principate, by frequently changing milder sanctions, from the prohibition against holding public office to varying terms of exile.[61] The death penalty for all other capital crimes was also disappearing; from the second century B.C., executions were increasingly avoided. This was done, in particular, by the use of procedural device: the accused, if a Roman citizen, was allowed to remain at liberty up to, and often even after, condemnation, and thus he was able to go into exile.[62] With respect to murder, which was the most frequent of capital crimes, Sulla went still further: about 81 B.C., he formally abolished capital punishment and imposed exile for all murder with the exception of parricide, and about twenty years later, Pompey removed even this exception.[63] Thus, in the period preceding the end of the Republic, the death penalty was hardly ever inflicted on Roman citizens.

The other harsh penalties of the past disappeared as well. Early praetorian edicts substituted payment of damages for talion.[64] Selling insolvent debtors and thieves into slavery abroad was abolished by, respectively, Lex Poetelia[65] and praetorian edicts.[66] The late Republic did not know corporal punishments; in particular, scourging wrongdoers was long past. Basically, it also did not know imprisonment, which was recognized "not as a punishment but only as a rough method of detention."[67] Thus, exile was the most severe of the still existing punishments. It meant that the culprit could not return to Rome without risking death and that, if the exile was for life, some or all of his property was to be confiscated (although the confiscation was enforced with varying degrees of effectiveness).[68] The other penalties included fines and payment of multiple damages, as well as loss of capacity to perform various public and private rights such as voting, holding public office, serving on the jury, representing others at courts, or being a guardian of minors. All these sanctions were fairly administered by a well-developed court system. In particular, the fairness with which the criminal jury-courts of the late Republic "afforded the accused scope for making his defense [was] most impressive and might even seem . . . exaggerated."[69] Thus, in the era of the highest development of Roman culture, leniency replaced the old severity of criminal punishments. Only later, under the imperial tyranny, did administration of justice display new harshness and cruelty.

MODERN EUROPE

A strikingly similar process occurred again, centuries later, in modern Europe, and then also in various European offshoots. After the fall of Rome, European societies began their growth from infancy; the new period of conspicuous cultural progress did not start until more than 300 years ago. To be sure, there were important developments during the Middle Ages and the Renaissance, such as scholastic philosophy and Gothic architecture, the socializing impact of the Peace of God, the growth of Italian cities and of commercial towns, and the artistic achievements of the Renaissance. However, each of these developments was of limited comprehensiveness and influence, and nowhere did all the three areas—science, arts, and, in particular, socialization—progress together to a degree comparable with that of Periclean Athens or Augustan Rome.

The great progress of Europe started with the rise, beginning in the seventeenth century, of modern science—that is, science unconstrained by authority and dogma, stressing experience over speculation, and pervaded by the idea of using scientific discovery for the improvement of the human condition. This last idea has paved the way for development of various practical disciplines inferring technical recommendations from the newly established theoretical claims of scientific knowledge. The resulting inventions produced, during the eighteenth and nineteenth centuries, the industrial revolution and the ensuing acceleration of unprecedented economic growth—from the economic takeoff in about 1800 in Britain to that in Prussia, France, and Austria and to the high-consumption economies of Western Europe and other industrial democracies of today. The needs of the growing economy and opportunities provided by the accumulation of wealth brought about progress in education—compulsory basic schooling and extended periods of further intellectual and professional training for the ever-growing labor force and managerial class—which implies further accumulation and widening spread of knowledge and ideas.

Economic growth and the spread of knowledge and ideas were among the major determinants of the political change—from absolute monarchies to modern democratic systems. This was a long and often difficult change. In England, preceded by the early reforms of 1641 and Oliver Cromwell's dictatorial Commonwealth, it led from the Glorious Revolution and the Bill of Rights to the firm establishment of parliamentary system and then to making the democracy more democratic through reforms extending the franchise. Between abolition of absolutism in 1789 and the introduction of a parliamentary republic after 1870, France went through a constitutional monarchy, a revolutionary republic, Jacobin tyranny, Napoleon's Empire, two further constitutional monarchies, four years of the Second Republic, and, again, a dictatorship; all this included four revolutions, three successful coups d'état, and fourteen different constitutions. Prussia experienced, in the early 1800s, limited liberal reforms, especially abolition of serfdom, strengthening of municipal self-government, and establishment of a modern court system. It became a constitutional monarchy in 1850, and the basics of its constitution were inherited by the whole of Germany in 1871. This was not a democratic constitution, but it contained many important democratic traits. Parliamentary democracy was established in Germany in 1919 to reemerge, after the Nazi period, in the Federal Republic. Other European societies have tended in a variety of ways in a similar direction, and, today, all nations of Western Europe live under democratic rule.

The implications of this political development for progress, as understood here, are immense. The removal of authoritarian constraints further stimulated the very development of economy that had itself helped to remove the constraints; and both the growth of political democracy and the increase of wealth have, also in feedback, promoted further accumulation and spread of scientific knowledge, which has made, since Galileo and Newton, most impressive strides. The same holds true with respect to the aesthetic indicator of progress. Freedom of artistic expression and growing resources have brought about the most diversified development of the arts, and the growth of egalitarianism has been conducive to their mass consumption, which became more widespread than ever before.

From the standpoint of this book, however, the most important influence of political change, as well as of economic and intellectual growth, has been in the field of socialization. The modern economic system became, to a degree unknown by earlier civilizations, a school for useful work and for fair commercial mores, and in the process, the economy has been helped all over continental Europe by the norms of civil law—a modernized version of the Roman law, whose stress on fulfillment of obligations, good faith, and decency of commercial habits has been mentioned earlier. The growth and eventual triumph of democracy brought about the most comprehensive training in the obligations and rights of citizenship. In this, the political system has been largely assisted by the system of education at all levels, higher education included; traditionally, the European university has functioned not only as the place for development of science and training of intellectual elites but also as an instrument for learning of socially useful attitudes. Furthermore, all three changes—political, economic, and educational—have been helpful in extending the borders of social solidarity, and there is some analogy in this to what had occurred in ancient Rome. In particular, the development of the worldwide economic market and the worldwide exchange of ideas, both supported by improvements in transportation and communications, have promoted the increasing acceptance, by the modern civilized individual of the basic unity of the human race.

Of course, the progress thus outlined was neither linear nor uninterrupted. As even this brief account should imply, the European nations have undergone in recent centuries many reversals because of wars, economic disasters, retrogressive coups, and revolutions. Nonetheless, on the whole, the progress of Europe—or of the western half of Europe, as of today—has been enormous. It has been outlined here briefly, its more detailed presentation would exceed the needs of this book. However, to fully appraise its scope, one should compare where we are today in Western Europe, North America, and a few other industrial democracies of European heritage with the level of development of the majority of other societies.

At the outset of this advancement, criminal laws were, again, severe. To be sure, like Draco's laws and the XII Tables, they were less severe than their predecessors, and one particularly important alleviation was the gradual disappearance, beginning in the twelfth century, of criminal liability without guilt and the reduction of penalties for negligent, as opposed to intentional, wrongdoing.[70] Nonetheless, the harshness was marked. *Constitutio Criminalis Carolina* of 1532,[71] the criminal code of the Holy Roman Empire, was still in force, at least basically,[72] in Austria, Prussia, and many other German principalities. It was pervaded by feudal tradition in its catalogue of crimes, procedure that relied on torture for obtaining evidence, and in particular in severity of sanctions. Thus, for instance, burning at the stake was the sanction for sorcery, arson, sodomy, and counterfeiting.

Depending on the gravity of their crime, murderers were killed by beheading, horse-dragging, tearing apart by claws, or breaking on the wheel. Treason was punished by dismemberment; stirring up disobedience, by beheading or flogging and exile; robbery, rape, abortion, and major brawls, by beheading. Aggravated theft, that is, theft by a burglar or anyone armed, was sanctioned by hanging, but in lighter cases the judge was free to impose exile preceded by gouging the eyes or cutting the hand off; for a common thief, if caught redhanded, there was exile preceded by pillory and flogging. For blasphemy, the judge had the choice of the death penalty or mutilation. False accusation that led to a painful punishment was sanctioned by talion. Women, when convicted for capital crimes, were drowned; however, a mother guilty of frequent infanticide was impaled and buried alive.[73] *Constitutio Criminalis Carolina* was not abolished in Prussia until 1794. In Austria, it was replaced, in 1768, by *Constitutio Criminalis Theresiana*, an almost equally harsh code, to be repealed nineteen years later.

Before 1789, the criminal laws of France consisted of *coutumes*—collections of customary laws recorded since the fifteenth century on—and royal *ordonnances* of the sixteenth and seventeenth centuries. Even though less systematic, these norms were, in many respects, similar to those of Germany and Austria. In particular, the lists of acts to be punished included, as under *Carolina*, not only wrongs against persons, property of others, and interests of the state, but also such medieval crimes as sorcery and blasphemy, as well as other kinds of all-embracing *lèse-majesté divine*. The procedure was inquisitiorial and tortures were systematically applied. The penalties were, in their cruelty, reminiscent of those German and Austrian: the death penalty was implemented by hanging, beheading, burning at the stake, breaking on the wheel, or quartering; and corporal punishments included cutting off or burning the hand, cutting off the tongue, the mouth, and the ears. The harshness of the system was increased by the judicial discretion to punish, by analogy, acts not listed by the law as crimes.[74]

The cruelty of the continental systems was in various respects matched by the law of England. This was an "extremely severe" law, especially in Tudor and Stuart days, during which time the list of capital crimes included about fifty kinds of acts ranging from murder and treason to repeated vagrancy, heresy, and witchcraft.[75] No contemporary statistics were kept, but according to a later estimate, at the end of the sixteenth century executions amounted to 800 per year.[76] Most of them were carried out by hanging. However, treason, if committed by a man, was open to drawing, hanging, disemboweling, and quartering; treason by women, as well as heresy, was sanctioned by burning; poisoners were boiled to death.[77] Punishments for some clergyable felonies and for misdemeanors included stocks, pillory, branding, flogging, and ear cutting.[78] Executions were public— to the excitement and often the enjoyment of the crowd.[79] The compulsory extraction of guilty pleas and confessions, especially in the Star Chamber and by use of *peine forte et dure*,[80] spelled not only procedural harshness but also danger of convicting the innocent.

In the last decades of the eighteenth century, the severity of European criminal laws started to decline markedly. The decline was, to a great degree, prompted by the ideas of Enlightenment. The ideas—a not always consistent mixture of rationalism, social contractarianism, belief in natural laws and natural rights, and humanitarianism, especially of utilitarian persuasion—were largely addressed to the criminal lawmakers. Beccaria, Bentham, Montesquieu, Voltaire, and many others demystified criminal punishment. Under their impact, educated opinion no longer perceived criminal punishment as an expression of hatred or penance for sin. The penalties became rational, teleological implements. The purpose of the punishment, particularly in the view of Beccaria, Bentham, and other utilitarians, was to minimize general suffering by preventing crime and to minimize the pain of criminals by imposing on them the smallest penalties needed for prevention. More specifically, since all human behavior is a rational outcome of the anticipated pleasure-pain calculus, criminal punishments should involve exactly the minimum of pain necessary to outbalance the gratification expected from the criminal act; they should never bring more suffering than the crime they sanction. Any excess over this measure would, as unnecessary suffering, run against the utilitarian stand. That is why the penalties in use should be mitigated and all cruel penalties abolished. This is particularly true with respect to all kinds of aggravated executions, mutilation, and humiliating and even corporal punishments. In Beccaria's view, non-aggravated capital punishment should also be removed.[81] And all the traditional cruelties of criminal procedure must disappear. These demands were directed to lawmakers, and especially to the enlightened despots of the time—"until the French Revolution, only they might have been expected to implement the idea of the humanitarian reform."[82]

Some of them did implement the idea. Pressed by her son, the future Emporer Joseph II, Maria Theresa of Austria mitigated in the last period of her reign the operation of the *Theresiana*, her own harsh code. According to data from the Czech part of the Empire, she pardoned 40 of the 50 criminals sentenced to death in 1778 and 44 of the 60 in 1779, and in secret (so they would continue as a deterrent) she instructed the courts not to enforce various cruelties prescribed by the *Theresiana*.[83] In 1787, under Joseph II, the *Theresiana* was replaced by a nearly modern criminal code. The code was pervaded by the ideas of Enlightenment: socially harmful behavior, not sin, was to be punished, and thus most religious and "victimless" crimes disappeared; the principle of equality before criminal law and the principle of individual guilt as ground for punishment and determinant of its severity became firmly established. And two years before the Declaration of the Rights of Man and Citizen, the principle *nullum crimen sine lege*—if not a law, no crime—was accepted; "which constituted . . . an arrangement of utmost importance for the later development of criminal law in Europe."[84] Conspicuously, most of the old cruel penalties were abolished, especially all kinds of aggravated executions, and moreover, the death penalty itself all but disappeared.[85] To be sure, some cruelties remained. Confinement was very harsh (with the inmates shakled to the wall in the most severe prisons). Public flogging was in use, as well as the pillory, branding of the most dangerous convicts, and towing boats on the Danube.[86] In the following years all these rigid measures disappeared. Branding, public flogging, and towing boats were abolished in 1790. The severity of prisons was somewhat alleviated in 1803, markedly so under the Criminal Code of 1852. The death penalty, reinstated in 1795 for high treason and in 1803 for aggravated homicide and forgery of currency, was afterward enforced with increasing rarity.[87] It was abolished in the Austrian Republic for common crimes in 1919,[88] and it was reabolished following the Nazi reversal.[89]

Frederick the Great of Prussia inherited the cruelties of the earlier German law (as embodied in the *Carolina*). In 1740, three days after his accession to the throne, he prohibited torture from nearly all, and somewhat later from all, criminal trials. By use of secret instructions to courts, he repressed aggravation of executions. He also limited, by decree, the list of capital crimes; in particular, all property crimes were removed from the list. With respect to the majority of the remaining capital crimes, he often pressed the courts in individual cases to refrain from imposing the death penalty; he also issued a great many pardons.[90] Consequently, execution rates were moderate: according to statistics from 1775–78, executions averaged 11.5 per year, the majority of them for various forms of murder.[91]

Besides all these changes, Frederick initiated extensive work on general reform of law. However, the new code produced by this work, the *Landrecht*,[92] was enacted only in 1794, four years after his death. The criminal law of the *Landrecht* was a compromise between Frederick's ideas and feudal influences revived in reaction against the French Revolution. Thus, the *Landrecht* inherited from the *Carolina* some of the (never formally repealed) cruelties, such as the wheel for treason or murder and burning for arson that caused lives to be lost. On the other hand,

Frederick's reforms and the impact of the Enlightenment appeared lasting in various respects. For the overwhelming majority of crimes, confinement replaced the death penalty of the earlier law. Moreover, the *Landrecht* came close to accepting the principle *nullum crimen sine lege*, personal guilt as ground for punishment, and equality before criminal law; and it abolished the majority of religious crimes.

In the wake of the turmoil and reversals of Napoleonic wars,[93] the trend toward fully modernized criminal law grew stronger, especially among legal scholars in the universities. After twenty-five years of draftsmanship and immediately following establishment of constitutional government, the new Prussian criminal code was enacted in 1851[94]—a product both of German scholarship and of ideas borrowed from French law. The code was much more humane than the *Landrecht*. Despite strong abolitionist pressures, the death penalty survived, but it was limited to treason, assault on the sovereign, and various kinds of homicide. All aggravated executions were removed. There emerged a liberal system of mitigating circumstances. The principle *nullum crimen sine lege* received full endorsement. Moreover, between 1846 and 1877, the inquisitorial procedure gradually disappeared. In 1870–71, the 1851 code was, with minor changes, reenacted as the law of the whole German Empire;[95] one of the changes, following a near-victory of the abolitionists,[96] consisted in a further limitation of capital punishment—this time to murder and to attempted murder of the sovereign. With some more revisions, the code survived both world wars. Except for the Nazi period, these revisions included further lightening of penalties such as replacement of short-term confinement by fines[97] and limitation of criminal liability of minors.[98] A mitigation of particular importance occurred after the Second World War. German abolitionists, traditionally influential, had been silenced in the Nazi years, but they eventually prevailed in Western Germany; Article 102 of the Federal Constitution, in force since 1949, totally abolishes the death penalty.

There were also a number of smaller European countries such

as Tuscany, Naples, Sweden, and Denmark where enlightened despots opened in the late eighteenth century the process of mitigation of criminal laws; subsequently, in all of them, this process continued under constitutional governments. On the other hand, in two of the largest nations, France and England, no enlightened despotism has ever emerged, and it was up to forces other than the monarch's will to press for legal change.

In France, the impact of the Enlightenment on criminal law and procedure, virtually nil under the *Ancien Régime*, became overwhelming after the Revolution. In 1789, the Declaration of the Rights of Man and Citizen pronounced the principle *nullum crimen sine lege*[99] and the presumption of innocence of the accused. The Declaration also proclaimed that "[t]he law should establish only penalties that are strictly and obviously necessary."[100] Consequently, the criminal code of 1791 reduced the number of capital crimes (from 115 to 32) and removed confinement for life and nearly all corporal punishments. The enactment of the code had been preceded by abolition of torture from criminal procedure, promulgation of equality of all before criminal law, introduction of trials by jury, and removal of joint liability of the criminal's family members.

The subsequent upheavals of the Revolution and war brought about the rise of repression; in particular, since the proclamation of the First Republic, the list of capital crimes, as well as executions, was again on the increase and culminated with Jacobin terror. Only after the establishment of the Directorate, and especially under Napoleon, did criminal law become more lenient. To be sure, the Napoleonic criminal code of 1810,[101] which, subject to many amendments, is still in force today, was in some respects harsher than its predecessor of 1791. This was largely due to Napoleon's impact; facing increase of crime under wartime conditions, he wanted to deter potential wrongdoers.[102] Thus, the penalties included imprisonment and death, as well as lifelong forced labor and banishment. Cutting off the right hand preceded execution for patricide, and for some other crimes, public pillory and branding were inflicted in addition to

confinement. Despite their harshness, these measures constituted only a limited reminder of the old-time severity; the basic,
humane traits of its 1791 predecessor were kept intact by the
Napoleonic code, "a criminal law of legality and egalitarianism,
based upon the moral responsibility of the offender."[103]

Since the July Revolution of 1830, the harshness has declined
further, although not without setbacks. Owing largely to widely
spreading liberal and neoclassical ideas, mutilation and branding
finally disappeared in 1832, the pillory sixteen years later. In
1832, these ideas, as well as unfounded jury acquittals (that is,
acquittals stimulated by harshness of punishments rather than
by innocence of the accused), brought about limitation of liability for all kinds of crimes by widely articulated mitigating circumstances.[104] This was followed, first, by moderation of penalties for political offenses, then by a general moderation of
punishments for a variety of common crimes in 1863,[105] and by
a gradual improvement of conditions in penitentiaries. In the
late nineteenth century, neopositivist criminology contributed
to a further change. Whereas "habitual" and "incorrigible"
wrongdoers were severely treated,[106] others enjoyed new leniency owing to introduction of parole. Moreover, criminal liability of juveniles underwent reforms: in 1898, confinement of
minors was partially replaced by outside supervision; in 1906, the
age limit of penal minority was shifted from sixteen (where it
had been since 1810) to eighteen; and in 1912, minors to age
thirteen became criminally not responsible, while punishment
of those over thirteen was partially replaced by education and
partially mitigated.[107]

This trend continued during the following decades, and after
World War II, it found strong, although indirect, support from
the New Social Defense movement.[108] Owing to that movement,
punishment of juveniles was replaced to a large extent by rehabilitation,[109] probation was introduced,[110] and the use of parole (supplemented by rehabilitative efforts) increased, however
unevenly.[111] To be sure, in the wake of each of the world wars
some new harsh norms were enacted to sanction a few crimes

perceived as especially dangerous; in particular, after 1945, aggravated armed robbery[112] and most severe crimes against state security were added to the list of capital crimes,[113] as well as infanticide (by anyone else than the child's mother) and cruelties that caused a child's death even if the death was not intended.[114] Despite these enactments, however, the long-term trend toward greater leniency has been continuing, not only in general, but also with respect to capital punishment. Until 1981, the death penalty sanctioned predominantly aggravated homicide, in contrast with the original, Napoleonic version of the criminal code by which the number of capital crimes exceeded thirty. And even though the just mentioned few items have been added to the capital list in recent decades, the law in action was overcoming the occasional new harshness of laws on the books: judicial discretion and executive pardon brought executions to a trickle. For instance, in the years 1950, 1953, 1956, 1959, 1962, and 1965, executions for common crimes[115] amounted, respectively, to 12, 2, 2, 1, 0, and 1.[116] The culmination came recently; on September 18, 1981, the National Assembly enacted total abolition.

On its face, the law of England was late in joining the club of the more enlightened systems. During the eighteenth and at the beginning of the nineteenth centuries, capital statutes were enacted profusely. In the preceding period, there were approximately fifty capital offenses.[117] According to Blackstone, in the 1760s the number of nonclergyable capital crimes amounted to 160,[118] and in 1819, Sir Thomas Fowell Buxton put it at 233.[119] This accumulation was partially artificial; to a degree, it consisted in splitting a transgression that should constitute a crime of one kind into a number of narrower capital crimes; for instance, "by a great number of statutes the forgery of different specified documents was made felony without benefit of clergy."[120] Nonetheless, the accumulation meant that the overwhelming majority of criminal offenses were capital, irrespective of their gravity—from murder and high treason to pickpocketing of twelve pence or more, destroying trees, and being in the company of gypsies,[121] and the old cruelty of aggravated executions was not abolished. Penalties for the few noncapital crimes such as fraud, libel, or battery were also severe; they included whipping, pillory, and sometimes mutilation or confinement in prisons that were "in an infamous condition."[122] No wonder advocates of a more enlightened legal system were complaining that the "extreme severity, instead of operating as a prevention to crimes, rather tended to inflame and promote them, by adding desperation to villainy."[123]

Still, the complaints were only partially justified—there occurred, in the period under discussion, a great increase in the harshness of criminal norms on the books, but it was outweighed by a clear decrease in their harshness in action. This was due to a changing perspective on the role of punishments. While in the preceding period of vindictiveness and stress upon repentance, penalties had been inflicted with great rigor, now a new philosophy became influential: criminal punishment is to deter from the largest possible variety of undesirable acts, and it deters best if imposed in an exemplary manner, that is, with great harshness, but not necessarily strictly. Consequently, through various mechanisms, the many harsh laws came to be enforced only occasionally. These mechanisms included, in particular, evasion of capital accusations by grand juries;[124] restrictive construction of capital statutes by judges;[125] convicting for an offense lesser than the crime committed, for instance, by understating the value of the stolen property;[126] merciful acquittals;[127] and the expanding commutation, through royal pardon, of death sentences to banishment overseas[128]—a device that, during the nineteenth century, largely replaced the disappearing benefit of clergy.[129] Also the basic fairness of criminal procedure, with its tradition of jury trials and more recent strengthening of the accusatory principle, became a factor of importance.[130] All these conditions contributed to an overall decline in punitive harshness, especially toward the end of the eighteenth century. This was particularly true with respect to the death penalty: total executions fell, in London and Middlesex, from 365 per decade in the mid 1700s to 220 in the 1790s to 104 in 1801–10,[131] and the ratio of persons executed to those capitally convicted fell from more than one in two in the middle of the eighteenth century to one in ten in the early 1800s.[132]

Despite this alleviation, very harsh penalties, in particular executions for minor offenses or aggravated executions, were still implemented, although occasionally, and their intermittent infliction spelled inconsistency and arbitrariness. These shortcomings contributed to the growth of a law reform campaign led by Romilly, Mackintosh, Fowell, Buxton, and other outstanding legislators and criminal policymakers[133]—a campaign that, on the one hand, was a reaction against the shortcomings, and on the other, a part of the long-lasting movement for the abolition of capital punishment stretching from 1750 to our own days.[134] The campaign, having influenced general opinion, provoked many mitigating changes in criminal law. Thus, various vestiges of earlier cruelties disappeared—aggravated executions for treason, the pillory, and then also banishment overseas. Since the 1820s, the severity of sanctions for various noncapital offenses declined as well. Moreover, conditions in prisons gradually improved under the impact of the prison reform crusade, which had been largely stimulated by John Howard's seminal inquiry.[135] Most importantly, the death penalty continued to give ground to milder sanctions. In 1826–32, Sir Robert Peel's Acts greatly diminished the number of capital offenses, and their list shrank further through the following decade. In 1841, there were only ten items on the list, and since 1861 the list has been limited to treason, murder, piracy with violence, and arsons at dockyards and arsenals. This meant, in practical terms, death for murder only, at least in peacetime; only during the world wars were a few nonmurderers executed in England.[136] Moreover, numbers of executions for murder continued to decline—in 1930–49, they averaged 10.6 per year.[137] Eventually, after the two-centuries-long struggle, the abolitionists won—in 1957 the Parliament further limited and, in 1965, eliminated imposition of the death penalty for murder.[138] Thus, basically without capital punishment[139] and with rather mild terms and humane conditions of confinement for major crimes, British criminal law is today, both on the books and in operation, at least as lenient as that of any Western European nation.

CHAPTER 5

WHY DOES THE LAW BECOME LESS HARSH?

The corroborative value of the preceding analysis seems clear; in all societies scrutinized, ancient and new, punitive harshness of criminal law has declined. This process is not self-explanatory, however. What are its determinants? In answer to this question, some changes in human motivation that occur in the course of social development should be specified. Then the process of declining harshness will become clear.

PRIMITIVE SOCIETIES

Since this analysis deals with the impact of social evolution on criminal law, only societies where criminal law has already emerged are of interest here.[1] These societies display a peculiar characteristic: the lower the level of cultural development of a society, the harsher the criminal penalties necessary to prevent its members from socially harmful behavior. In particular, barbarian and early postbarbarian societies, where fear rather than moral aversion constitutes the main motivation against wrongdoing, need powerful means for avoidance training. To meet this need, criminal punishments must be very harsh; and so they are, as indicated by the history of early Greek and Roman law, by laws of medieval Europe, and by the laws of other primitive peoples of ancient and recent times.

What these harsh penalties provide is powerful aversive training. Primitive lawmakers, in particular those of the distant past, did not know the theoretical principles of aversive instrumental learning. They were, however, applying these principles intuitively, and the following comments should make it clear how ingenious this intuitive application was.

There are two kinds of aversive instrumental learning—direct and vicarious. (Attractive instrumental learning may be divided into the same two categories, and many of the following comments are relevant to it, but for obvious reasons it is not of interest to criminal law.) Vicarious learning is particularly important for these considerations. It results from observation of behavior of others and its consequences for them; by "observation" I mean witnessing, reading about, or listening to descriptions of the experiences of others. Observation of noxious consequences brings avoidance of similar conduct on the part of the observer. Experiential data demonstrate that effectiveness of vicarious punishments frequently matches, and sometimes exceeds, that of the direct ones.[2]

How does aversion from punished behavior emerge in man? Preponderant evidence implies that it emerges in two partially interdependent ways. It emerges, first, in the course of a trial-and-error process, owing to more or less "automatic" association of behavior with its immediate consequences, and, second, from an awareness of the outcomes of our behavior: we become conscious of noxious outcomes of behavior X, memorize them, and then select avoidance of X for future occasions.[3] The former, associative mechanism has been inherited by us from our animal ancestors, whereas the latter, cognitive, is, at least in its most advanced form, specifically human.[4]

There are various prerequisites for efficacy of aversive instrumental learning. Two of them are of particular importance. The first is simple—it consists in sufficient intensity of punishing events, that is, in sufficient intensity of direct punishments and sufficient perceived intensity of those vicarious. In most circumstances the increase in intensity makes learning more effective,[5] which matches our ordinary experience—the stronger the punishment, the greater the fear.

Proper scheduling of punishments constitutes the second prerequisite of effectiveness. Punishment may follow behavior X certainly or intermittently. The former means that whenever X happens, punishment follows. The latter means that punishment is interspersed with nonpunishment or even with reward (e.g., answering a child's tantrums sometimes by hugging and on other occasions by spanking).

It is a well-established fact that the two processes just outlined, associationist and cognitive, operate under the certain scheduling of punishments; thus, certain direct punishments of behavior X, as well as its vicarious punishments perceived as certain, bring aversion from X. This holds true, in particular, with respect to punishment of instrumental responses:[6] if the punishment of a response instrumental in producing reward is certain (or perceived certain, when it is vicarious), it brings aversion, provided that it is strong enough to overwhelm the reward. On the other hand, intermittent punishment of an instrumental response does, rather unexpectedly, reinforce the punished behavior, not suppress it. The response that had been intermittently punished is more resistant to elimination (by subsequent certain punishment) than behavior that had never been punished at all.

This inferiority of intermittent punishment in producing aversion finds some corroboration in various nonexperimental studies: delinquency has been found correlated to capricious parental discipline,[7] and intermittent punishments that had been applied to extinguish children's dependent behavior apparently increased its strength.[8] More importantly, the inferiority has been clearly demonstrated in numerous experiments on humans and on animals alike.[9]

This discovery has been explained by Amsel and others: the intermittently applied punishment becomes a classically conditioned cue for the impending, nonpunished instrumental acts.[10] To be sure, this inferiority of intermittent punishments holds within certain limits only; if intermittent punishment is so powerful as to produce truly shocking aversion, it may sometimes have permanent suppressive quality even if it happens only a few times or once.[11] Nonetheless, at least basically, certain punishment is clearly superior.

In conclusion, there are two major prerequisites for the effectiveness of aversive instrumental learning: severity of punishment and its certainty. For vicarious punishments, this means perceived severity and perceived certainty, and these perceptions may differ from reality—an issue to which I return soon.

Criminal laws of primitive societies meet both prerequisites. The punitive severity of these laws has already been discussed. Many of these laws also provide public infliction of torture and public executions and thus additionally increase the degree of vicariously aroused fear. Moreover, through public infliction the cruelties may arouse, at least in some observers, aversion powerful enough to offset the impact of the occasional intermittence of punitive measures.

The intermittence is occasional only; in a primitive society, the degree of perceived certainty of punishment is high. This is so for several reasons. First, these are societies made of relatively small, predominantly rural groups in which everyone knows and watches everybody else. Consequently, the chance that a lawbreaker may escape apprehension is less than in modern, anonymous life. Second, the limitation of liability to those guilty is unknown; when criminal law emerges in primitive societies, it accepts absolute responsibility, that is, responsibility independent of the age of the lawbreaker, his intent, and sanity. Thus, exoneration of negligent or accidental acts (too difficult to comprehend and thus appearing to constitute intermittence[12]) was unknown in the periods preceding Draco's legislation, the XII Tables, and *Constitutio Criminalis Carolina*;[13] and so was, in medieval Europe, the distinction between the culpability of right-minded adults and the innocence of children and of the insane.[14] Furthermore, other, largely supernatural measures make primitive punishment look certain:

a potential offender usually knows in advance . . . that if his offense is not detected by men in the usual way, various gods will take care of it; priests with their auguries and other magic means, or forces of nature—e.g., some animals or plants will denounce the offender; or a deity will demask him on trial if he fails to admit his guilt, [especially on] trial by ordeal.[15]

Since perceived severity and perceived certainty of punishments are, at this level of social development, essential for effective vicarious training, many of these measures work as adaptive tools. They do not have to be used with awareness of their functional character; for instance, the medieval courts, when applying trial by ordeal, probably believed that they were using reliable means of evidence and did not know that, in fact, they were providing a false impression of perfect punitive certainty in a way beneficial for arousal of aversion. Still, at that period, the arrangement was a useful and ingenious sociopsychological invention, and so were some of the other means just mentioned.

To be sure, not all these means were useful. In particular, the degree of severity of punishments was not necessarily optimal; apparently, the sanctions were often harsher than necessary for the most effective avoidance training. This was so, first, because, even for a rational lawmaker implementing the principles of instrumental learning with full consciousness, it would hardly be possible to find out exactly how harsh is harsh enough to effectively deter. Furthermore, cruelty of some primitive lawmakers—especially of tribal tyrants and ruling elites immersed in class struggle—accounts for more harshness than necessary. This may be the reason why we sometimes discover, when comparing primitive societies on a similar level of development, that while in one of them punishment for a crime is very severe, in the other it is even harsher and very much so. For instance, in the Athens of Draco, an insolvent debtor was to be enslaved, whereas under the XII Tables the creditors had the right to kill him and divide his body.[16] However, as long as fear is the main motivation against socially harmful behavior, this surplus of harshness does not hurt the preventive effectiveness of the law; punishment harsher than necessary to effectively deter is as useful for deterrence as punishment that is exactly harsh enough.

CIVILIZED SOCIETIES

The Change of Motives: From Fear of Sanction to Moral Aversion. The utility of the primitive harshness of criminal laws fades in the course of social evolution. As indicated earlier, evolutionary progress consists, among other things, in men's becoming better socialized; they increasingly avoid harming others in the society, and they perform with increasing effectiveness what is socially useful. This modification of human behavior is brought about by changing human motivation. The changes in motivation of progressing societies are complex and diversified. They often include rising rationality prompted by the spread of knowledge; rising influence of economic motives prompted by industrial development; and emergence of the mixture of mental experiences, called sometimes "achievement motivation," which is a vague blending of pride, vying for prestige, fear of failure, etc. Of all these and other changes, one is especially significant for avoidance of harmful behavior. This is the strengthening and spread of moral experiences that gradually replace fear of sanction as the main stimulus against wrongdoing.

Moral experiences are easy to define. They emerge in us in response to ideas of conduct that is being evaluated as intrinsically right or wrong (i.e., right or wrong per se without reference to any purposeful rationale). If the ideas are of present or future conduct, the moral feeling is an experience of duty.[17] If this is the feeling of one's own duty, it has driving properties; it stimulates demanded and inhibits prohibited acts.

For the most part our moral experiences are weak. They emerge as dispositions rather than as actual drives and are often below the threshold of consciousness; the majority of us do not steal or cheat, and we do pay debts, almost automatically. Counteraction may, however, make them powerful. If someone counteracts them, for example, tries to persuade us in earnest that we do cheat, commit incest, ridicule in public the disability of a sick person, or are cruel to someone helpless under our care, our feelings of duty not to do so become clear and strong. Similarly the provocation, such as reading about or witnessing cruelties inflicted by others, arouses the feeling of duty to help the victims, and in the case of the cruelties committed by nations or governments, the duty to fight a war or a revolution.[18]

This change of human motivation—the increasing replacement of fear by morality—is useful; moral aversion provides a motivation clearly superior to fear. Of course, it is more appealing; we prefer those who refrain from wrongdoing because of the feeling of duty. More importantly, for several reasons it is stronger and more reliable. First, fear of sanction prevents crime only as long as the threat operates. Second, even in the presence of the threat, the daring are more effectively prevented from wrongdoing by belief in its immorality than by fear. Furthermore, fear of sanction works best as a deterrent for only one portion of criminal behavior—commitment of calculated acts, like professional theft or killing for hire; unpremeditated, highly emotional behavior, like killing in a sudden anger, is much less deterrable. On the other hand, internalized aversion effectively prevents both calculated and emotional wrongdoing.

It is due to this change in human motivation that the old harshness of criminal law in a civilized society becomes not only unnecessary but also harmful, and the more so the more developed the civilized society is. Why is this the case? For answer, the role of criminal law itself in the very process of the strengthening and spread of moral experiences must be scrutinized.

The Role of Criminal Law. We acquire our moral experiences in the process of social learning. The process operates in two ways. First, it works through persuasive communications on what behavior is right and wrong, on what one should and should not do. These communications come from the society we live in. Thus, with the aid of gestures, facial expressions, example, and especially language, each of us acquires the evaluations from those with whom we interact: originally from parents, then from childhood and school peers, and then from an increasing number of others, in individual and group contacts, and in such symbolic encounters as family, religious, or national ceremonies. This simple mechanism is responsible, in any social group, for development of its morality (that is, of any morality, whatever the morality recommends or forbids). Thus, the mechanism was, in particular, responsible for the strengthening and spread of the morality of Athens, Rome, and modern European societies, especially of the moral attractions to useful and aversions from harmful behavior. The way in which this mechanism has operated—within kinship groups; in the agora and forum; through the word of philosophers, priests, and writers; in schools and political clubs; through modern mass media and all other channels—should be clear in the light of the earlier comments.

The second mechanism is a peculiar variation of the first; it also consists in persuasive communications. However, these are persuasive communications of a special quality; they are expressed in the form of rewards and punishments—more specifically, rewards explicitly contingent upon a behavior evaluated as intrinsically right and punishments explicitly contingent upon a behavior evaluated as intrinsically wrong. This is how, in general, parents or schools reward children for acts of sacrifice or helpful courage and punish them for lying or cheating. This is how the army responds to similar acts of soldiers, and various churches to the acts of their members. The rewards and punishments vary: gifts and culinary treats, honors and promotions, the promised salvation, acknowledgment and friendliness on the part of the rewarding agents are among the former. The latter include verbal rebuke and spanking; loss of rights, privileges, and honors; constraints of freedom; future pains in hell; withholding affection; and the like. All of them have one common characteristic: when applying them, the rewarding or punishing agent makes it clear that they are being applied for behavior that ought to have been done as right or ought to have been avoided as wrong. Consequently, their application works in a dual process: as an implement of persuasive communication and as an implement of instrumental learning or, briefly, as an implement of "persuasive instrumental learning." Thus, if effectively applied, they bring attractions and aversions with peculiar emotive tone: a feeling of duty to do what is right and a feeling of duty to avoid wrongdoing. This is how, owing to persuasive instrumental learning, moral experiences are acquired.[19]

Persuasive instrumental learning of moral experiences has been implemented in the progressing societies, past and present, by a variety of rewarding and punishing agents such as families, churches, schools, and various peer, professional, and other groups. As indicated earlier, the rewards and punishments of developing economies were also a major influence, as well as rewards and punishments following various acts of political participation in the societies that moved away from authoritarianism. However, one powerful influence is of utmost importance for these considerations; norms of law, especially of criminal law, may be most helpful in promoting the acquisition of morality. Addressing the society at large, the norms of criminal law may reinforce moral experiences of all of us, especially of potential lawbreakers, by the process of vicarious persuasive instrumental learning—the observation, mostly indirect, of criminals being punished for the crimes.

To operate in this manner, criminal punishments must meet two important requirements. The first constitutes a universal prerequisite for effectiveness of any aversive instrumental learning, direct or vicarious: punishments must be perceived as certain, and the preceding general discussion of the issue is fully relevant here. The second requirement is that criminal punishments be persuasive as moral communications; they must impress everyone that wrongdoers are being punished because their behavior was intrinsically wrong. This can be effectively done only if the punishments match the moral sentiment of the society, that is, under three conditions: the punishments must be imposed for behavior widely perceived as wrong; they must be applied with the degree of severity widely considered as right; and they must be applied consistently, that is, in accord with the principle "Treat like cases alike." In the comments to follow, it will be convenient to call punishments that meet these three conditions "just punishments." (That is, of course, an arbitrary denotation—"justice" here means consonance with the dominant moral views rather than any absolute quality of the acts thus labeled.) It is clear that punishments that are unjust in the sense accepted here have no persuasive power. For instance, if an American court punishes someone for being a good Samaritan or applies an extremely harsh measure for petty encroachment or selects for punishment the only black from among a large group of those proved to have committed an identical offense, no one will be persuaded that the behavior is being punished because it was wrong. To be sure, an unjust punishment can result in aversion from punished behavior, especially owing to the fear of sanction. The aversion will, however, be void of the specifically moral emotive tone—with no persuasive moral power, the punishment cannot bring about the experience of duty.[20]

Did punishments imposed by criminal laws operate effectively as moral reinforcers in the progressing societies of the past? The inference from the just outlined theoretical stand is clear—whether and how effectively they did depends on how certain and how just they looked. Thus, they could not have been effective under those tyrannical systems where autocrats have imposed clearly unjust sanctions, especially punishments for behavior not perceived by the society as wrong or punishments perceived as unjustly harsh or cruel. Neither were they effective under those legal systems where, as in eighteenth-century England, punishments were highly uncertain and inconsistent.

On the other hand, there are no grounds to question the educative effectiveness of criminal law whenever punishments were just and reasonably certain. To be sure, there is no way now to demonstrate that the moralizing impact of punitive certainty and justice was a major determinant of the low criminality in much of nineteenth-century Europe; it is impossible *ex post facto* to trace motivations preventing wrongdoing, to control influences other than criminal law, and owing to scarcity of statistical data, even to ascertain the exact past crime rates of the majority of the European nations. However, the limited information we do have is not in the least inconsistent with the idea of criminal law's reinforcing morality. For instance, in England, until the early 1800s, under the most uncertain and capricious system of criminal punishments, crime was pervasive and growing,[21] whereas rectification of these flaws during the subsequent decades has been followed by a marked decline in criminal behavior, especially since the middle of the century. And this was how, in 1786, after a few decades of new certainty and justice of criminal law, Leopold of Tuscany summed up his experience in the introduction to his famous Code:

With the utmost satisfaction to our paternal feelings, we have at length perceived, that the mitigation of punishments . . . , together with a certainty . . . of punishment to real delinquents, has, instead of increasing the number of crimes, considerably diminished that of the smaller ones, and rendered those of an atrocious nature very rare.[22]

THE EXPLANATION

The foregoing considerations provide the explanation for which we are looking. Owing to the psychological mechanisms of persuasive communications and persuasive instrumental learning, the moral aversion against wrongdoing intensifies and spreads in progressing societies. It thus not only becomes powerful but also gradually replaces fear as the main stimulus against harmful behavior. In this way the relative impact of the two stimuli—fear and morality—changes; whereas at a low level of social development members of the group are prevented from wrongdoing predominantly by the fear of sanction, the feeling of duty becomes the main motive of the civilized man. To be sure, this is always only a partial replacement: even in the most developed societies the fear of sanction plays a role, but the role becomes increasingly secondary. As indicated earlier, this change in motivation is useful; moral aversion provides a motivation superior to fear.

This growth and spread of moral aversion as the main motive against wrongdoing, largely produced by the criminal law itself, makes the inherited severity of penalties unnecessary; there is no need to use the harshness of a prior era while—in the words of the late Chief Justice Warren—"the evolving standards of decency . . . mark the progress of a maturing society."[23] This uselessness of the harshness is likely to be perceived by the society. This means that the harshness is perceived as infliction of unnecessary suffering by a group of people who have increasingly learned not to harm others. In this way the severity inherited from the earlier period is perceived as unjust (that is, becomes unjust in the here accepted sense of justice): the population experiences the duty on the part of the legal system not to impose penalties of such harshness. To clarify this point, a simple mental experiment may be of use. Torture and public executions still caused delight in a large proportion of Europeans in the seventeenth and eighteenth centuries (and public executions were known in the United States through the last century), but the civilized reader of today would be disgusted by the very idea of their reintroduction, and the disgust would be predominantly moral.[24]

By being unjust, the surviving harshness is also harmful from the legal policy standpoint. First, it destroys persuasive instrumental learning; unjust criminal punishments are void of persuasive moral power. Furthermore, unjust punishments seem to be counterproductive: "Seeing inequitable punishment may free incensed observers from self-censure of their own actions, rather than prompting compliance, and thus increase transgressive behavior."[25] This harmfulness is often perceived or at least intuited by the public, as implied by many critical pronouncements that have come from various progressing societies. For instance, "the minds of people are corrupted" by the excessive severity, claimed Montesquieu in *The Spirit of Laws*;[26] and in Beccaria's view, the severity "emboldens men to commit the very wrongs it is supposed to prevent."[27] "You shock virtuous men by an appearance of . . . wide disproportion between the offense and the penalty," complained Dr. Samuel Parr, criticizing the harshness of the English law at the outset of the nineteenth century; "you run the hazard of weakening . . . general respect for . . . the laws" and you may "induce the offender to stand absolved in his own mind from the common laws of morality."[28] "If the society considers a penalty as unjustly harsh, its application . . . brings sympathy and friendliness for the offender" in the words of Petrażycki. These feelings may easily become "extended to the prohibited acts themselves; which undermines disgust for crime and, sometimes, even results in glorifying the criminal and in favoring harmful behavior."[29]

These two experiences—the feeling of injustice of the inherited harshness and the perception of how harmful this harshness is—provide the explanation we are looking for. They make it clear why there emerges, in progressing societies, the demand to make the penalties more lenient. This demand accounts for the general tendency toward declining severity of criminal law. In this way the tendency can be explained by a rather simple psychological mechanism.

FORCES LIMITING THE DECLINE OF HARSHNESS

What has been explained here is only a tendency, not an exceptionless "law" of declining severity. Thus, it is not true that, whenever a major step in social evolution is made, a decline in severity of criminal punishments ensues. The decline in severity is an indirect outcome of cultural progress. It follows directly only the change of the law in force, most notably the legislative change, and also such changes as more lenient judicial and prosecutorial practices or wider use of executive pardoning power.

For this legal and, especially, legislative change to result from an advancement of culture, some intermediate steps are necessary, and they may be lacking.

The first of these steps is the articulation of the idea of the legal change. More specifically, some individuals must grasp and publicly spell out that the former harshness constitutes unnecessary suffering and is, therefore, unjust; that by being unjust, it harms the operation of criminal law; and that, being unjust and harmful, the harshness should decline. To be effective, these assertions must influence those who make the laws. How can this influence be implemented? This depends largely on the political system of the progressing society and, especially, on who the lawmakers are. In societies where the laws are made by the general population or its substantial segment or by their representatives, the general population or those enfranchised must be persuaded that the change is needed. If such a society is small, the idea of the change may be spelled out by its proponents in direct interaction with all relevant members of the group: the elders or the soldiers or all adult male citizens, such as those assembled in the *Ekklesia* of Athens. If, on the other hand, it is a large and complex representative democracy, the proponents of the legal change must employ much organized effort and use various means of mass persuasion. The more democratic the progressing society, the better the chance that the idea of reducing the severity will win the minds and hearts of the population and thus force the lawmakers to comply.

However, one should not overestimate the effectiveness of the democratic process. In particular, it is not true that in societies where an open flow of ideas is possible, socially useful ideas always capture the general sentiment; to believe so would come close to the familiar fallacy of universal functionalism.[30] A variety of counteracting forces such as wars, internal conflicts, economic difficulties, malfunctioning of governmental agencies, especially of the criminal justice itself, as well as impact of demagogues, may be the reason why, even in an open society, the uselessness of a prior severity will not be widely perceived and will not arouse general and strong enough moral disgust to bring about the desired legislative change. Some of these forces not only prevented the decrease but also caused a temporary increase in punitive harshness in the history of progressing societies such as eighteenth-century England or France in the years following each of the world wars.[31]

Nonetheless, if lawmakers depend on (or directly express) the popular will, the chance for a decrease of punitive harshness is clearly higher than under autocratic regimes. Wherever a despot is the ultimate lawmaker, he must be convinced that the previous harshness is not only unhelpful but also brings useless suffering and that useless suffering is wrong. Sometimes convincing him is feasible; a few enlightened despots of the eighteenth century were persuaded by Beccaria, Voltaire, Montesquieu, and others. However, the majority of the despots known to human history have been neither enlightened nor benevolent, and many of them were pleased rather than appalled by inflicting needless pain. This explains why authoritarianism often promotes not only punitive harshness but also cruelty. Montesquieu apparently had this in mind when claiming that "in all, or almost all governments of Europe, penalties have increased or diminished in proportion as those governments favored or discouraged liberty;"[32] a related idea was expressed by Durkheim.[33] This claim should not be pushed too far. Democracy does not make the decline of harshness certain, nor does despotism make it impossible. But there is much merit to the claim: the chance of the decline's following cultural progress is much higher in an open society.

Such are the social forces that counteract the decline in punitive harshness. Some of them will be scrutinized in the following chapters. Owing to these forces, the decline in harshness has not been monotonic in progressing societies; there is only a tendency, not a law of declining harshness.

PART THREE

CAPITAL PUNISHMENT IN AMERICA

CHAPTER 6

THE ABOLITIONIST TREND

THE NINETEENTH CENTURY

The preceding chapters provide an explanation for the abolitionist trend that culminated in America on the eve of *Furman*. In the United States, the cultural evolution produced, as in the ancient world and modern Europe, a tendency toward decline in punitive harshness, and the abolitionist trend became a particularly visible component of this tendency.

The years following the American Revolution had already brought about some mellowing of criminal laws in the original thirteen states. Much of colonial law had been brutal, even though less so than the contemporary laws of England and of continental Europe. Corporal punishment was used profusely, especially stocks, pillory, flogging, branding, ear cropping, and castration of slaves in Virginia and North Carolina. To extract confessions, torture was allowed, albeit with limitations.[1] The lists of capital crimes were much shorter than in Europe. Nonetheless, the seventeenth century had seen theocratic capital laws in New England and the Mid-Atlantic colonies with witchcraft, blasphemy, and idolatry sanctioned by death, and on the eve of Independence, Virginia penal laws listed 70 capital crimes for slaves.[2] Torture death never took hold in the colonies, but some cases have been reported,[3] and slaves were sometimes burned at stake, the last of them in 1773.[4]

Enactment of the Eighth Amendment constituted a response of the Founding Fathers to the primitive crudity of the past. The amendment, patterned after the British Bill of Rights of 1689, was adhered to much more stringently than its predecessor, under which the British had been torturing convicts for more than a century.[5] In conjunction with like provisions in the states' constitutions, this norm became an important symbolic force and a catalyst for the later decline in punitive harshness.

To be sure, the Eighth Amendment prohibited torture, not death. In 1791, the death penalty was written into the federal law and laws of all the states in the Union, and the Fifth Amendment explicitly acknowledged its validity.[6] Nonetheless, in the decades following the Revolution, the idea of total abolition was conspicuously present in the United States: "Early Americans were also heirs of the European Enlightenment and its trenchant criticism of vengeful criminal laws and capital punishment in particular."[7] Under the impact of Montesquieu, Bentham, and especially Beccaria, some of the best minds in America launched an attack against the death penalty with Benjamin Rush, Benjamin Franklin, and Thomas Jefferson among the early proponents of abolition.

Their struggle was pursued through the entire nineteenth century by increasing numbers of abolitionists of various persuasions. Among them were lawmakers, from Robert Rantoul and Marvin H. Bovee to Newton M. Curtis at the very end of the century; judges and officials of federal and state governments, with William Bradford and Edward Livingston among the most outstanding; and a multitude of dedicated clergymen and religious leaders, educators, journalists, and men of letters. To spread contempt for the death penalty, they used all kinds of persuasion: oral addresses and sermons, treatises, pamphlets, novels, poems, articles in professional periodicals and in common press. They were, moreover, organizing groups not only to influence the general population but also to press the lawmakers. The antigallows societies emerged and spread from the 1830s on, first in the Eastern States, then to the frontier. The individual abolitionists and the societies flooded lawmakers with petitions. And within the legislatures themselves, groups of abolitionist lawmakers were establishing abolitionist committees, the Rantoul committee in Massachusetts and Bovee's committee in Wisconsin being among the most renowned.[8]

The arguments of the abolitionists varied, some of them reflecting the instantaneous mood of the day and many others reflecting a much more durable stock in trade of the abolitionist ideology. "I shall ask for the abolition of the punishment of death," Jefferson is quoted to have said, "until I have the infallibility of human judgement demonstrated to me."[9] Livingston also stressed the danger of executing the innocent.[10] Since Rush and Bovee, the opponents of capital punishment have challenged the belief in its deterrent power, that is, its deterrent power stronger than that of confinement. Rush insisted that the death penalty does not deter murder, and it actually stimulates murder in those who, being suicidal, crave to be executed.[11] He also stressed the demoralizing impact of executions on the general population: they "lessen the horror of taking human life."[12] Phrenological evidence was used to prove that "faulty cerebral organization, not conscious choice, was the cause of criminality."[13] The Quaker proponents of rehabilitation of wrongdoers blamed the death penalty for its obvious incompatibility with the rehabilitative ideal.[14] Rantoul and other adherents of the natural law doctrine perceived the death penalty as an infringment of inalienable individual rights.[15] Charity, love, and compassion were used as an argument against punitive harshness, especially capital punishment, by many religious and lay abolitionsits and by men of letters such as Whittier and Simms. Some of them also stressed the intrinsic sanctity of human life[16] and the cruelty to the convicts awaiting execution.[17]

The practical outcomes of this campaign were understandably uneven. During the major part of its first century, the United States was too diversified to generate uniform cultural progress resulting in a uniform change of criminal law; there was too much cleavage such as that between the North and South, the

East and the shifting frontierland, the free and the slave, the offspring of the colonists and waves of immigrants. Thus, in the 1800s, the campaign was differentially effective.

Enactment of abolition, then and now, was the campaign's most conspicuous effect. Legislatures of six states abolished or nearly abolished the death penalty between 1846 and 1897, but in three of them, Iowa, Maine, and Colorado, the abolitionist mood was shallow enough for the penalty to be promptly restored; in Maine reabolition soon followed restoration.[18] Only in Michigan, Rhode Island, and Wisconsin has abolition, introduced respectively in 1846, 1852, and 1853, never been repealed.

Reducing the lists of capital crimes was much more widespread than abolition. Pennsylvania became an early pioneer by limiting, in 1794, capital crimes to first-degree murder. (This was a return to the state's colonial tradition; Penn's criminal law of 1682, limiting the death penalty to premeditated murder, had been replaced by the British with a much harsher code in 1718.) Subsequently, many other states shortened the catalogues of capital crimes, and on the eve of the Civil War, most of the Northern and Eastern states had only a few capital crimes on their law books—treason and murder among the majority, and one or two other offenses, which differed from state to state. The South was much harsher, especially with respect to slaves, but even there, the catalogues were shrinking. In South Carolina, the catalogue gradually declined from 165 items in 1813 to 22 in 1850.[19] In federal law, by 1897, the number of capital crimes had fallen from 60 to only treason, murder, rape, and military offenses under the articles of war.[20]

There were also some further important limitations adopted by an increasing number of state laws. One of them consisted in the introduction of statutory degrees of a given crime, only the utmost degree, such as first-degree murder, being capital. Another one consisted in a steady though slow transition—between 1838 and the pronouncement of *Furman*—from the mandatory to the discretionary system of death sentences.[21] The transition had a double meaning. On the one hand, removal of mandatory death sentences spelled mitigation of relentless harshness. On the other hand, it was a practical response to pervasive evasion of law; since colonial times, juries had been acquitting the guilty whom they did not want to send to the gallows.[22] Later, prosecutors also started exercising evasive control. Thus, by removing mandatory executions, the harsh law on the books was yielding to a practice that reflected milder attitudes of the society.

These attitudes found reflection in further changes both on the law books and in how the existing laws were administered. In particular, exonerating and mitigating circumstances, such as insanity, juvenile age, and self-defense, were increasingly alleviating punitive harshness, as was the widely emerging right to appeal convictions.[23] In some states, liberal use of executive pardon was limiting infliction of the death penalty,[24] and when the penalty was to be inflicted, efforts were made to soften its harshness by making executions swift and painless and, since the 1830s, by gradually removing them from public view.[25]

All these were marked alleviations. However, they stopped clearly short of total abolition. Apparently, the level of development of nineteenth-century America was not high enough for the abolitionist idea to take an overwhelming hold on human minds and thus to force the removal of capital punishment. Only the accelerated progress of our century, especially in its later part, was to endow the idea with new influence.

THE TWENTIETH CENTURY

The idea of abolition simmered through the first few decades of the twentieth century, expanded in the 1930s, and became powerful in the 1950s and 1960s. Its many carriers—individuals, pressure groups, mass media[26]—were using the old and adding new arguments in its favor, and the old arguments were often restated with new sophistication. Thus, in line with Jefferson's and Livingston's concerns, abolitionist societies, judges, scholars, prison administrators, and state officials worked to provide evidence that the death penalty always carries the risk of executing the innocent[27] and that the risk consists not only in killing someone other than the actual lawbreaker but also in killing a lawbreaker whose blame was either none or mitigated because of insanity or age or other circumstances that the court failed to take into account.[28] Bovee's claim, apparently influenced by Beccaria, that capital punishment does not deter better than long-term confinement, has become fashionable in recent decades and has stimulated a wealth of statistical inquiries aimed at its testing. Despite their increasing refinement, the inquiries have been inconclusive;[29] we do not know, and we may never learn, whether capital punishment deters more effectively. But this lack of knowledge prompted a new argument on the part of many abolitionist utilitarians: the death penalty is so hurtful and brutal that strong reasons for its imposition must be made clear and certain. Thus, the burden of proof of its utility—in this case its deterrent utility—is placed upon its advocates, and unless they provide the evidence, the penalty should be abolished.[30]

The brutality of the penalty has been stressed with new vigor and in a variety of ways. Descriptions of the suffering of convicts have been widely circulated in general and professional literature.[31] Among them are vivid reports of executions—of "extreme evidence of horror, pain, strangling"[32]—an experience claimed to be so "brutally degrading" that "[i]f those alone who have participated in an execution could vote on the death penalty, it would be abolished tomorrow."[33] There are also descriptions of the cruelty of waiting, often many years, on death row[34] and of those particularly moving cases where the exceptional pain of the convicts or their deeply human characteristics or doubts about their guilt are likely to arouse the readers' indignation.[35] Furthermore, the old theme of the brutalizing effect of capital punishment, which especially undermines society's "respect for the sanctity . . . of human life," has been emphatically stressed again,[36] as has its negative impact on administration of criminal justice, especially through "acquittals . . .

not merited by the accused [as well as] convictions and executing not justified by an unemotional consideration of the evidence."[37]

Some further arguments have been added to the list, and since they reflect broad social concerns, their influence has been strong, sometimes stronger than justified by their validity. Among the concerns reflected, there is a range of social ills in America. A variety of professional and amateur criminal etiologists have claimed that these ills constitute the main determinants of criminal behavior. From this claim they jump to the radically deterministic conclusion that the criminal, ridden by social (and psychological) forces he is unable to control, has no choice but to break the law. Consequently, ascribing guilt to him is nonsense, and punishing him, especially punishing him harshly, is both morally wrong and purposeless, and this is, of course, particularly true of punishing him by death. How can anyone be sent to the gallows for having bad parents, being born in poverty, growing up in a slum, or being discriminated against? The more so that all these and many other criminogenic influences have been brought about by the general society, that is, by all of us; we are at fault rather than the criminal whom we produced. How, then, can we, the guilty society, kill him, the innocent victim of our institutions? The only humane and reasonable policy would be to abandon sanctioning crime and to remove the root causes, in particular, all the social ills that generate crime—poverty, economic inequality, racial discrimination, family irresponsibility, and others. This view has been frequently pronounced by large numbers of journalists, clergymen, politicians, lawyers, and social philosophers,[38] and its influence is widespread. According to a 1966 survey, "most Americans believe that crime can be curbed better by positive measures that attack the environmental and psychological roots of criminal activity than by great employment of police force."[39]

Two further, widely accepted ideas are related to this stand—the idea of rehabilitation and the idea of equality before criminal law. The advocates of rehabilitation claim that since social and sociopsychological influences make a criminal, they can also be ingeniously used to unmake him; unmaking the criminal should be considered the main purpose of criminal justice. This re-educative notion has been with us since the Pennsylvania Quakers, but it reached its heyday in the 1960s, largely under the impact of psychologists and psychiatrists, especially those of psychoanalytical persuasion.[40] Whether the idea means making the criminal better or more rational or permanently scared or cured from "aberration" is neither clear nor agreed upon among its proponents. Whatever its meaning, one of its implications is important here—the death penalty has been denounced as "the antithesis of the rehabilitative . . . orientation of twentieth century penology."[41]

Since the 1950s, egalitarianism, and especially equality before the law, has become a pervasive social and legal concern, and it was a major theme of the Warren Court's constitutional activity. From this perspective, the death penalty has been forcefully denounced for its inequitable application, which has been disproportionately frequent against the underprivileged, especially the poor and the black. The disproportion has been explained by ignorance and helplessness of the poor (who cannot "afford the best legal talent to defend" them[42]) and by racial discrimination,[43] especially in the South.[44] And even unbiased capital conviction has been called "so haphazard in its execution as to be grossly inequitable."[45] It should be clear, in the light of the preceding *Furman* analysis, how many of these arguments found their way into the Supreme Court.

First, however, these arguments found their way into the minds of an increasing proportion of the general population. In a public opinion poll conducted four times between 1953 and 1966, a sample of respondents from all over the United States was asked: "Are you in favor of the death penalty for persons convicted of murder?" The percentile distribution of the answers is as follows:[46]

Year	For	Against	No opinion
1953	68	25	7
1960	51	36	13
1965	45	43	12
1966	42	47	11

A more generally worded question—"Do you believe in capital punishment (death penalty) or are you opposed?"—produced, in 1965, 38 percent retentionist vs. 47 percent abolitionist replies (with the remaining 15 percent undecided).[47] An identical distribution of replies was prompted, in 1966, by a somewhat more specific question: "Some states have abolished capital punishment—executing persons who commit a murder—and have substituted life imprisonment instead. Do you favor or oppose capital punishment?"[48] Thus, in 1965–66, the abolitionists emerged, for the first time, as the majority of those voicing an opinion, and there was within this majority a substantial core of energetic, determined, and deeply committed crusaders.

The practical outcomes of this change were diverse and far-reaching. To a degree, they emerged on the law books. The number of abolitionist states grew; between 1957 and 1965 the lawmakers of six states[49] abolished, and the lawmakers of two more states nearly abolished, the death penalty. In two states the abolition came in 1972 by decisions of state supreme courts.[50] Furthermore, transition from mandatory to discretionary death sentences continued, especially for murder, to sweep, before the mid-1960s, nearly all jurisdictions in the United States.[51] However, the most dramatic change occurred, not on the law books, but in the capital laws in action; since 1947 on, rates of executions have rapidly declined.[52] (reducing)

The decline occurred in a number of ways. One of them, illuminated by numerous court cases, was the increasing hesitation on the part of trial courts to pronounce death sentences;[53] the jurors, as well as trial judges, are part of the community, and they are not immune to a change in the community's moral sentiment. Shortage of past statistical data makes it impossible to estimate precisely how much the number of death sentences pronounced all over the United States has declined during the past decades. But we at least know that "[t]here were fewer admissions to death row in the 1960s than executions in the 1930s, despite a comparable absolute number of homicides in these two decades."[54] In particular, there were 105 admissions to death row per year on the average from 1960 through 1968[55] and "167 executions per year on the average during the 1930s. . . . And, of course, the latter figure excludes commutations."[56]

The decline of executions has been due only partially to the changing attitude of the trial courts. Whereas in 1960–68 the courts were annually sending between 86 and 118 convicts to the death row,[57] the total numbers of executions declined in a nearly linear way from 56 to 1960 to 0 in 1968.[58] Thus, there must have been ways of eliminating executions other than the reluctant stand of juries and judges.

The most conspicuous of these other ways was bringing capital convictions under an increasingly aggressive appellate review. The aggressiveness was largely due to a concerted action of abolitionist lawyers, especially those of the NAACP Legal Defense and Education Fund (with Amsterdam, Greenberg, and Meltsner among the most dedicated ideologues, organizers, as well as defenders in individual court cases).[59] During the 1960s, they developed an ingenious strategy. They appealed, with some success, every capital conviction. When unsuccessful on appeal, they asked for a writ of certiorari. If turned down by the Supreme Court, they petitioned the federal district court for a writ of habeas corpus. If the petition was rejected, they appealed to the federal court of appeals, and, whenever unsuccessful, they again sought a Supreme Court hearing. They also applied for postconviction remedies to the state trial courts and courts of appeals with another potential resort to the Supreme Court of the United States.[60] In this manner they aimed at reversing some executions and stalling all others, that is, at bringing about a *de facto* moratorium. They expected that once many hundreds of convicts were logjammed on death row, these convicts would be eventually spared by executive clemency if not by legislative action, since "there were very few governors who wished to preside over mass executions."[61] As implied by earlier comments, this anticipation was only partially correct—lives of these convicts were eventually spared, but they were spared by the Court in *Furman* rather than by commutation.

Besides the appellate review, two further mechanisms were

helpful in eliminating executions. One of them was, indeed, the practice of executive pardon. This was, however, an implement of limited impact; in 1961–68, the average annual number of commuted death sentences throughout the United States amounted to less than 17.[62] Another influence, much more effective than the clemency, consisted in administrative behavior of state penal authorities who were, especially during the 1960s, increasingly reluctant to schedule and perform executions.[63]

These were the mechanisms that, owing to the new atmosphere surrounding the death penalty, brought about the decline and eventual disappearance of executions. As just indicated, there were 153 executions in America in 1947, whereas between 1960 and 1968 the annual numbers of executions declined steadily from 56 to 0;[64] after 1968, there were no executions for several years. (Consequently, as anticipated by the abolitionist lawyers, the death row population was swelling, from 189 in 1960[65] to 642 on the eve of *Furman*.[66]) Thus, even though many laws on the books still provided for the death penalty, the living law seemed to have entirely removed it. It is no wonder that the belief in total abolition's being just around the corner was spreading. "The death penalty appears to be reaching the vanishing point,"[67] it "is on its way out,"[68] claimed those anticipating the impending abolition, and they repeatedly expressed hope that Aaron Mitchell, gassed in California in April 1967, would "enter the annals of crime as the last man to have been legally executed in the United States."[69]

These expectations centered predominantly upon the Supreme Court. To be sure, they might have materialized through legislative action, and indeed, lawmakers were pressed for enactment of total abolition, not only at the state, but also at the federal level.[70] However, because of the slowness and unwieldiness of the legislative process, the abolitionist pressures would have to be truly powerful to win in both the Congress and in all states. On the other hand, for the Supreme Court to bring about the change, only a consensus of five men was required, which is the bare majority of the Justices.

A number of constitutional provisions such as the Due Process or Equal Protection clauses might have been used by the Court as grounds for the change, but none of them was as suitable as the Eighth Amendment's prohibition against cruel and unusual punishment. Originally enacted to prevent torture, the prohibition (as well as its counterparts on states' constitutions) had been used, through its slowly broadening interpretation, to outlaw an increasing variety of sanctions. Thus, in 1910, the prohibition was used to outlaw the sentence of 12 years in chains at hard labor as a sanction too harsh for forgery of a document,[71] even though "relative cruelty" of this sort was clearly not within the original intent of the Framers. Court reports have also been full of attempts to reduce, as "cruel and unusual," prison sentences perceived as excessively long. These were, however, attempts of limited success; the courts have displayed "reluctance to substitute appellate for trial court judgment on the amount of punishment."[72] In 1958, denationalization was held cruel and unusual as involving "the total destruction of the individual's status in organized society."[73] Four years later, in *Robinson v. California*,[74] the Court held the Eighth Amendment applicable to the states and extended the prohibition on imprisonment for being addicted to narcotics. The long-lasting efforts to use the prohibition against brutalities of prison life, unsuccessful under the traditional court doctrine of a "hands-off" policy regarding prison administration, became more effective in the 1960s; in particular, these efforts brought about limitation in the use of solitary confinement,[75] flogging,[76] aversive therapy,[77] as well as extension of the prohibition on lack of medical care[78] and on disgusting conditions of the prison as a whole.[79] Also various ways of performing executions have been challenged on the basis of the Eighth Amendment—death by firing squad,[80] lethal gas,[81] electrocution,[82] second electrocution after the first failed to kill,[83] etc. From all this, there was only a short distance to the idea of challenging the death penalty as cruel and unusual per se, that is, of using judicial power, especially of the Supreme Court, to implement the total abolition.

The idea has been spelled out in literature,[84] and in 1963 it was spelled out within the Court itself in Justice Goldberg's dissent from a decision not to review an appeal.[85] In 1969 the Court for the first time heard the argument that capital punishment was offensive to the Eighth Amendment, but by reversing the conviction on another ground, the Justices avoided dealing with the issue.[86] The subsequent developments within the Court are familiar. *Furman* ended inconclusively, and in the wake of *Gregg*, not only has the death penalty been reconfirmed on the law books, but also, since 1977, executions have emerged again. Thus, the expectations that had been running so high did not materialize; during the 1970s, there was a dramatic reversal of the abolitionist trend. Suddenly, the development of the American law turned against the general tendency of social evolution. Why did the reversal occur, and how lasting will it be? These questions are dealt with in the following chapters.

CHAPTER 7

WHY DID THE REVERSAL OCCUR?

As these considerations show, the reversal was eventually implemented by the Supreme Court. This implementation can be explained by a fairly simple chain of events. The Justices, not immune to the general sentiment, acted under its influence, and the general sentiment had suddenly changed; the abolitionist sentiment reached its peak in 1966, but it has undergone a steep decline since then. This decline was, in turn, caused by the spreading anger about crime and the fear of crime. The anger and the fear were generated by an increasing pervasiveness of crime, and the pervasiveness was an outcome of the progressive worsening of administration of criminal justice. Hence, in the ultimate analysis, the reversal of the abolitionist trend is perceived here as an indirect reaction against the decay of the criminal justice system.

This chain of events is dealt with now. It is examined in the reverse order, from the *explanans* to the *explanandum*. I proceed from the decay of the criminal justice system to the growth of crime, to the anger and fear, and eventually, to the decline of the abolitionist sentiment as the most immediate determinant of the legal reversal under discussion. In the light of this analysis, a cautious, tentative prediction of the future of capital punishment in America will become feasible.

CRIMINAL JUSTICE

A criminal justice system can effectively prevent crime. To do so, it must be skillfully organized. If it is not, and if strong criminogenic forces operate in a society, the society will be pervaded by crime. In this sense, deficiencies of a criminal justice system cause crime, and a well-organized criminal justice system constitutes a necessary condition for crime control.

All this is just commonplace. Nonetheless, this set of truisms runs against the stand preponderant among criminal etiologists of various persuasions. Their views, some of them radically deterministic, have been mentioned above.[1] Largely disregarding the impact of criminal law, they look for the broad social (and sometimes psychological or biological) conditions that determine criminal behavior. They also believe that once we have discovered the social determinants of crime and of its growth, we may be able to remove them and thus implement prevention.

Proponents of this stand suggest a variety of explanations: Lombrosian atavism, destructive forces of the Freudian Id, bad parents and broken families, bad companions, war, poverty, inequality, discrimination, ignorance, private investment property, anomie, and many more. The logical structure of these conjectures varies. Some have been intended as exceptionless explanations of all kinds of crime while others are explicitly probabilistic; some claim to be true any time and place while others know their own historical limitations. Their cogency varies as well. But, whereas a few are too vague to be tested (e.g., the Freudian) or have been proved false (e.g., the Lombrosian), many more constitute valid statistical generalizations. In particular, many studies, American and foreign, confirm that bad parents and broken homes are associated with various kinds of later wrongdoing, and so are living in the company of criminals, and, at least in some societies, discrimination, poverty, or growing up in deprived urban areas.

The belief that removal of these and similar social determinants of criminal behavior constitutes the best crime prevention policy has been widespread in this country and proclaimed by scores of legal policymakers. For instance: "We will not have dealt effectively with crime until we have alleviated the conditions that stimulate it," and this means an "action designed to eliminate slums and ghettos, to improve education, to provide jobs;[2]" "The only way . . . to abolish crime is to . . . [m]ake fair conditions of life. . . . Abolish the right of private ownership of land, abolish monopoly;[3]" "If we are to control crime, we must undertake a massive effort to rebuild our cities and ourselves, to improve the human condition, to educate, employ, house and make healthy."[4]

However widespread, these proclamations are ill advised. To be sure, efforts to solve the broad social problems and the suffering they bring are most worthwhile for obvious reasons and irrespective of whether the suffering generates criminal behavior (the more so that some of these problems are more acute than the crime itself). But an attempt to control crime exclusively or mainly by solving these problems is hopeless.

First, the degree to which persistence of criminal behavior depends on each of these problems is unclear. In any society the term *crime* denotes many kinds of very different behavior. Owing to this heterogeneity, the number of social determinants of criminal behavior is almost unlimited, even at a close level of the causal distance, and it grows while we draw back along the causal paths. That is why the social problems listed here constitute but a small fraction of the many determinants, and it is dubious whether solving them would prevent all or even the majority of crimes.[5]

However, even if removal of all these social ills were effective in preventing crime, we would be unable to remove the majority of them anyway and none of them easily and quickly. In particular, in view of the amount of crime in the United States, it is hardly possible to insulate everyone from associations with criminals and juvenile delinquents. It is equally impossible to "supply the missing 'parental affection' and restore to the child consistent discipline supported by a stable and loving family."[6] However much anomie, as claimed by Merton, may be responsible for a large proportion of criminal behavior, it would be difficult to abolish the meritorious democracy with its stress on achievement and upward mobility. If the Marxists had been correct—if a radical change of the socioeconomic system had been able to bring a crimeless society—it would be difficult to convince the American public that we can implement the ideal without destruction of free institutions. Thus, the attempt to solve the crime problem by removing broad "social causes" of criminal behavior is utopian.

To implement an effective crime prevention policy within a reasonable time span, a much narrower device is needed. The device is obvious: it consists in proper use of criminal law. Again, its proper use eliminates the "causes" of crime as much as any one of the social reforms just mentioned. After all, the poverty of justice administration is an important "cause"—a factor contributing to many, if not all, kinds of criminal behavior. Removal of this "cause" is easier and safer than a sweeping change of all criminogenic social institutions.

How can criminal law prevent crime? According to believers in its preventive potential, criminal law can do so in one or more of four ways: through deterrence, moral education of the society at large, incapacitation, or rehabilitation. Among the four, the latter two are clearly secondary. Incapacitation is intentionally limited; it aims only at preventing recidivism and only of those apprehended. Rehabilitation, that is, reeducation of apprehended wrongdoers, though equally narrow, has proved an attractive notion; as indicated earlier, the idea has long been with us. Unfortunately, the idea does not work well; in the current state of knowledge of human behavior, we do not know how to rehabilitate large numbers of wrongdoers,[7] even though we may sometimes succeed in this or another case. "With few . . . exceptions, the rehabilitative efforts that have been reported so far have had no appreciable effect on recidivism," complains the most penetrating analyst after surveying the major empirical studies of the 1950s and 1960s.[8]

Thus, of the four ways by which criminal law prevents crime, only two are of major importance: general deterrence and the society's moral education. Both mechanisms were touched on earlier, as well as their changing relative utility—the greater utility of deterrence at the lower and of moral education at the higher levels of social development. It was also stressed that this was only a change in degree of utility, not a total replacement of fear as a useful tool. Thus, even in the most advanced civilizations, fear of punishment hinders some potential wrongdoers from crime (a contention that is as obviously true as any truism is). However, this role of fear becomes, in the course of social progress, only auxiliary, and that is why, to effectively prevent crime in a highly developed society like ours, criminal punishments should promote moral learning rather than deter.

To be effective as an implement of moral learning, and in this way to optimally prevent crime, criminal punishments must fulfill two conditions specified earlier. First, they must be certain, or at least perceived as certain, which in an open, contemporary society means nearly the same;[9] if they are not, they tend to reinforce rather than suppress the punished behavior and thus lose the educative, as well as deterrent, power.[10] Second, they must be just, that is, widely experienced as just, according to the here accepted understanding of "justice"; if they are not, they will never persuade potential lawbreakers that breaking the law is wrong.[11]

Criminal punishments in America do not meet these prerequisites; they are neither certain nor just. To be sure, perfect certainty—punishment of every crime committed—would be a utopian ideal (with rather chilling political implications). Only an approximation of the ideal is feasible. However, the approximation is not being achieved in the United States at all. There are various forces responsible for this.[12] By far the most important of them is the almost unbridled discretion on the part of those who administer criminal justice, especially courts, prosecutors, and police. The discretion results in widespread nonenforcement of criminal law. Thus, not only is criminal punishment intermittent, but also it constitutes a very rare response to crime. According to estimates emerging from 1976 and 1980 statistics,[13] about 20 percent of the total amount of the crimes reported by the FBI (that is, crimes of particularly dangerous quality[14]) result in arrest of a suspect, and about 9 percent in conviction. Well more than one-half of convicted criminals immediately go on probation. Moreover, since a substantial part of criminal behavior, especially of minor offenses, goes unnoticed by the police[15] (with disbelief in effectiveness of law enforcement as the most important reason for nonreporting by the victims[16]), the crimes punished constitute an even smaller fraction of all crimes committed. Hence, "the proportion of actual offenses that result in prison sentences is . . . commonly estimated as being 1 percent of the total number of actual crimes committed, although it varies from crime to crime."[17]

There are a number of reasons for this leniency in exercising discretion. Some of them are ideological, and they should be clear in the light of earlier comments. It is claimed that broad social problems cause crime and to prevent crime, we must remove these problems rather than deal with symptoms by punishing criminals. It is also claimed that we should rehabilitate rather than punish. These ideas have had a long-lived and growing influence on enforcement of our criminal laws, an influence that reached its peak in the 1960s. The other reasons are practical. The amount of crime is increasingly overwhelming. Thus discretion and nonenforcement are expedient—if the police face too many suspects, it is convenient not to apprehend them; if those apprehended are too numerous to be tried by courts, it is convenient, through plea negotiations or other processes, not to try them; and if too many have been convicted to be accommodated in prison, it is convenient to let them go. Whatever the reasons, the implications of this policy are clear: the intermittence of criminal punishments tends to reinforce criminal behavior instead of extinguishing it.

Justice is also largely absent from the system. Again, unrestrained discretion is the major culprit; it makes punishment arbitrary.[18] The arbitrariness occurs in all steps of the criminal process from arrest and arraignment to decisions on granting parole.[19] It is most conspicuous, however, within the framework of plea bargaining—a practice that encourages defendants to plead guilty and, thus, to consent to conviction without trial in return for mitigation of the sentence. Traditionally performed "under the table," this bureaucratic expediency received formal recognition recently.[20] Today, it accounts for nearly 90 percent of all criminal convictions[21] and therefore deserves a few comments.

There are many deplorable outcomes of this practice (called long ago "a farce and travesty upon justice"[22]) such as infringements of the defendant's rights and of basic procedural fairness, prosecutorial and sometimes even judicial abuse, and confusion of roles of participants in the criminal process.[23] However, one of the outcomes is most unfortunate: plea bargaining makes criminal punishment inconsistent. Under this practice, lightening the sentence within discretionary boundaries does not necessarily result from insignificance of guilt or any other uniform principle but depends largely on how all the participants have played the negotiating game.[24] Dismissal of some of the multiple charges is often equally arbitrary. Reduction of charge means application of an arbitrarily selected criminal norm that has not been broken at all. The arbitrariness results in inconsistency; the negotiated penalties differ, in like cases, from case to case, judge to judge, and court to court. The basic requirement of justice—treat like cases alike—is gone, and thus gone is the just character of criminal dispositions.

Two extremes of the arbitrariness are particularly striking (and neither can be easily avoided despite the new trend toward making plea bargaining more open and structured). The first consists in convicting innocent defendants. Plea bargaining increases the risk of their conviction, and the convictions seem occasionally to occur;[25] this amounts not only to injustice by treating like cases differently but also to injustice in "absolute" terms. The other, very frequent extreme consists in letting the criminal go free, on probation or otherwise, without any rationale except expediency.

However haphazard the negotiated penalties are, they are subject to some regularities that make them even more unjust. First there is a more-than-chance probability that a negotiated penalty will be harsher than average if the defendant is guilt ridden, or ignorant, or poor. There are several reasons for this. One of them is that, owing to his feeling of guilt, an occasional defendant may plead guilty without considering any negotiations. An ignorant defendant may not know about the possibility of bargaining or misunderstand how the bargaining process operates.[26] If the defendant is too poor to make bail, he may be kept in pretrial detention, which greatly diminishes his bargaining power. Moreover, he may be unable to hire a private attorney, and public defenders are handicapped in the pursuit of some bargaining strategies, for example, delaying tactics or judge shopping.[27]

On the other hand, there is a more-than-chance probability that the worst offenders will be rewarded by the most excessive leniency: a "professional and habitual criminal . . . generally [has] expert legal advice and [is] best able to take full advantage of the bargaining opportunity."[28] He not only uses every available procedural device but also feigns "an appropriate . . . degree of guilt, penitence and remorse," to make his hearers believe "that he is contrite and thereby merits a lesser plea."[29] Moreover, he often uses informing as an important bargaining chip, especially informing on his accomplices. This information and possible testimony are useful to law enforcement. Hence, if he is motivated by remorse and by an acceptance of responsibility, it is meritorious of him to painfully break the loyalty to his friends for the greater social good. However, the information provided by him is self-serving. The repentance is not there, the loyalty to the society has not been restored, and whatever loyalties he has had to his friends and accomplices he breaks to make a better bargain for himself.[30] Consequently, the more shrewd and ruthless a criminal is, the better he is served by the administration of the "negotiated justice."

Do judges, by imposing negotiated penalties, tell anyone that defendants are being punished for wrongdoing? They convict "[a]rmed robbers . . . of attempted assault in the third degree; car thieves with unauthorized entry into a motor vehicle; child molesters with loitering in a school yard."[31] The judicial decision seems to convey to the defendant a mean message: you are being rewarded for yielding your constitutional rights, for having a shrewd lawyer, for your ruthlessness and ability to take advantage of the sale of sentences for pleas; or you are being penalized for not being cooperative enough, for being too poor to hire a good lawyer, for being too decent or too naïve to bargain ruthlessly and make the best deal possible. As a result, it is at least dubious whether negotiated punishments sound as moral communications at all; even if they do, their unjust character makes them void of persuasive moral influence and in this way destroys whatever educative power they might and should have.

These are the main reasons why criminal punishments, by being most uncertain and largely unjust, have been contributing to the accelerating growth of crime in America.

THE ANGER, THE FEAR, AND THE SUPREME COURT

The growth of crime has been shocking in recent decades. Reported violent crime has more than tripled since the late 1950s.[32] In particular, reported murder and voluntary manslaughter grew from 5.1 per 100,000 population in 1960 to 10.2 in 1980; forcible rape, from 9.6 to 36.4; robbery, from 60.1 to 243.5; and aggravated assault, from 86.1 to 290.6. This means, in absolute numbers, 23,044 persons murdered in 1980, 82,088 women raped, 548,809 persons robbed, and 654,957 violently attacked,[33] and since, with the exception of murder, the estimated total amount of crimes committed is about twice as high as of those reported,[34] these numbers should be doubled to reflect truly the scope of criminal behavior in this country.

The direct costs of crime include loss of life and limb, loss of earning capacity by those disabled, physical and mental suffering by the victims and their families, and extensive loss in the victims' property; the aggregate property losses resulting from reported robbery, burglary, and larceny alone approach $6 billion per year.[35]

The indirect costs are more complex. The pecuniary costs exceed $24 billion a year spent on police, courts, and prisons;[36] expenditure on private guards, detectives, and security devices; defense costs of those accused and, after conviction, welfare assistance for their families; indirect business losses, for example, inflated insurance premiums and loss of business patrons in high-crime areas. (Altogether the estimated direct and indirect economic losses amounted, in 1974, to $90 billion;[37] today the figure would, of course, be higher.)

The growth of crime results in spreading anger and fear. Both are stimulated, not only by direct encounters, but also and mainly vicariously by the flow of information about crime, especially information disseminated by mass media—television, periodicals, and the daily press provide regular coverage. For instance, during the first ten days of July 1981 (that is, in the period when these words were written) three widely read newspapers, none of them particularly sensational—the New York *Times*, Chicago *Tribune*, and San Francisco *Chronicle*—were treating their readers, every day, with information on crimes, criminals, and victims. The long list of the reported wrongdoing included, among others, street gang and school violence, gangland slayings, mayhem, a variety of brutal murders, hit-and-run killings, holdups and kidnappings, robberies, thefts, fraud, white-collar crimes, importing and peddling drugs, child abuse, vandalism, bombings, arson, batteries, and rapes. Much of this information was alarming. For instance, there was a description of a Los Angeles drug-related case in which "two couples found slain in a Laurel Canyon home were beaten to death with a blunt instrument."[38] Just before midnight, "a Bronx man, fatally stabbed [by an adolescent] staggered through eight subway cars

. . . and collapsed outside the motorman's cab."[39] In New York, in a "series of throat-slashings that left two vagrant men dead and 13 wounded," a 32-year-old suspect with a bloodstained razor was seized.[40] In Bradley, Illinois, the body of a 5-year-old girl "was found buried under a pile of trash. . . . She had been molested with a stick and bludgeoned to death."[41] After midnight, a Times Square mob of about 40 bottle-throwing teenagers mugged, robbed, and stripped naked a passerby and chased him to his death on a subway track. In the words of witnesses, "they had nothing better to do. . . . They did it to have fun."[42] This list of instances could be lavishly extended.

How can one react to events like that if not with fear, anger, even hatred? And, indeed, these seem to be the spreading reactions. They, in turn, precipitate new claims for toughness addressed to the administration of criminal justice—demands that harsher penalties be inflicted on wrongdoers and, especially, demands for capital punishment. In this manner, the feelings of anger and fear provide an essential link between the growth of crime in America and the rising attractiveness of the death penalty. However, there is confusion about the relative impact of each of these two feelings.

The fear of being victimized by crime constitutes an aversive experience. It is often painful and sometimes destructive. It also infringes upon freedom and life habits of those who go through it. They take burdensome precautionary measures, feel compelled to stay off the streets, become distrustful, abandon social contacts, and tend to turn, in a way that atomizes the society, into "mere . . . calculators estimating their . . . own chances for survival amidst their fellows."[43] Thus, it is easy to accept a commonsense guess that fear has been fully responsible for the increasingly punitive attitudes of the American public, which is ever more eager to control crime, and the guess has often been accepted.[44] However, in the light of the factual data at hand— both time-series data and cross-sectional surveys—the guess may meet approval only with a major qualification.[45]

The all-American time-series data show, first, the increase of fear of being victimized. Various indicators of fear (none of them perfect, to be sure) were used recently in the public opinion polls—indicators such as the feeling of being unsafe at home at night[46] or buying new locks or a dog or a gun for protection.[47] However, only one indicator has been used systematically since 1965, with the same question asked many times. The question was: "Is there any area right around here—that is, within a mile—where you would be afraid to walk alone at night?" This is a somewhat limited question—the respondents were asked only about the fear for themselves and not of their families' being victimized. Nor were they asked about the intensity of their fear. Nonetheless, the answers show a long-run (even though not linear) increase of fear, from the low point of 31 percent of respondents afraid in 1967 to 42 percent in 1979.[48]

The increase of punitiveness has been even more marked. Again, to measure the punitiveness, various indicators were used in the public opinion polls, but only two of the indicators have been used systematically with the same (or nearly the same) questions asked over many years. The first question was: "In general, do you think the courts in this area deal too harshly or not harshly enough with criminals?" The second question was: "Are you in favor of the death penalty for persons convicted of murder?" Whatever the degree of precision of both questions, the proportion of advocates of greater harshness of the courts grew, in a nearly monotonic way, from 48 percent of the respondents in 1965 to 85 percent in 1978.[49] The proportion of advocates of the death penalty for murder grew from the low point of 42 percent in 1966 to 66 percent in 1978.[50]

Since the increases in fear and in punitiveness coincide, it is easy to assume a simple causal relationship between the two.[51] Cross-sectional surveys disprove this assumption. Since 1965, proponents and opponents of harsher courts have been asked about their fear of walking at night, and so were, since 1970, proponents and opponents of the death penalty for murder. If growth of fear had been the only or the main cause of rising punitiveness, the punitive attitudes among those unafraid would have stayed unchanged or nearly so. In fact, however, the proportion of the punitive respondents increased considerably among both the afraid and the unafraid.[52] To be sure, since 1973, the increase was higher among those afraid of being victimized, but it was only slightly higher.[53] Presumably, the increase was also only slightly higher among those afraid about the safety of their families. Accordingly, the growth of fear, even though demonstrating some impact, cannot be perceived as the main determinant of the increasingly punitive attitude of the American public.

This conclusion finds some further support in another set of surveys. Between 1973 and 1977, the proportion of advocates of the death penalty in America grew from 60 percent to 67 percent of the total population.[54] Both in 1973 and 1977, an all-American sample of respondents was asked: "Suppose it could be proved to your satisfaction that the death penalty was NOT more effective than long prison sentences in keeping other people from committing crimes such as murder; would you be in favor of the death penalty or would you be opposed to it?" Those in favor amounted to 35 percent of the sample in 1973 and 46 percent in 1977.[55] Consequently, in both years, the majority of retentionists were not motivated just by fear and the resulting desire to prevent crime; and this was an increasing majority—it grew, between 1973 and 1977, from 58 percent to 68 percent of all the death penalty supporters.[56]

If not fear, what is the main determinant of the new punitiveness? There are reasons to believe that it is an increasing anger. The public opinion polls show that only a minority of this country's population, however considerable it may be, experience the fear of crime.[57] On the other hand, the great majority of us, that is, nearly all those able to sense the moral experience as described earlier, feel, when witnessing grave crimes or reading or hearing about them, moral indignation—the emotion of wrongfulness, outrage, often disbelief ("how could anyone have done anything like that?"), compassion for the victims, and a resulting anger if not hatred; and these feelings are the stronger the more abominable the wrongdoing is. If some of the above descriptions borrowed from the daily press were presented here in as much detail as they appeared in the newspapers, they might serve as mental experiments; when reading them, many of us would discover how strong the indignation and the anger are. These seem to be the feelings responsible more often than fear for the increasingly punitive mood, irrespective of whether they are called, by those who experience them, anger, hatred, revenge, or more respectably, desire for retribution or for "just desert."[58]

In this way, with anger and, to a minor degree, fear as its main determinants, the punitive attitude has been spreading in America.[59] Some indicators of its spread were mentioned here; the proportion of those in favor of greater judicial harshness has grown in a little more than a decade from 48 percent to 85 percent, and the share of supporters of capital punishment for murder, from 42 percent to 66 percent of the total population. (A differently worded question—"Do you believe in capital punishment . . . or are you opposed?"—disclosed a 38 percent advocacy in 1965 and 67 percent in 1977.[60]) The just mentioned increase in the proportion of those who opt for capital punishment for nonutilitarian reasons—that is, irrespective of whether it helps in reducing crime—is another symptom of the more punitive mood. Still another and, indeed, a striking symptom is the steep rise, between 1973 and 1977, in support for mandatory capital punishment: the proportion of those in favor of mandatory death sentences for murder grew from 28 percent to 40 percent and for killing policemen or prison guards, from 41 percent to 49 percent.[61] This far-reaching change in the general sentiment has been accompanied and reinforced by the publicized opinions of increasingly numerous advocates of punitive harshness—journalists, lawyers, politicians, policy proponents, and policymakers.[62]

These views could not but influence the Court through a variety of ways[63] and thus influence its decisions. To be sure, the Court is generally perceived as the branch of government least responsive to the public will. The Justices enjoy a unique degree of prestige and independence. Moreover, in a clash between their construction of the federal law and the views of the majority, the traditional American fear of the majority's wielding too much power works as a force restraining the majority itself. Accordingly, for the public will to overcome the stand of the Court may require a time-consuming struggle, as well as compromise. However, in the long run, when opposed by clear and strong sentiment of the majority, the Court has no choice but to eventually concede. Its power, and especially the implementation of its decisions, depends on the other branches of the government, which, in turn, depend more directly on the electorate; hence, the Court's power might be impaired if the Justices went too far too long in opposing the will of the nation on an important issue.

There is, however, more than political expediency here. Whether the death penalty is with us is largely perceived as a moral issue. Moral evaluations spread through the process of persuasive communications coming from the society in which we live—each of us becomes "contaminated"[64] by the views of others about what is right and wrong, about what should and should not be done. The Justices of the Supreme Court play a peculiar role in this process. On the one hand, they are particularly effective as communicators; because of their prestige and visibility, they influence the moral attitudes of others more effectively than nearly anybody else. On the other hand, however, they are a part and parcel of the broader society, and that is why they are themselves not immune to the persuasive power of the widely spreading evaluations they hear and read about.

All this explains the stand of the Court in the 1970s. *Furman* was argued in January and decided in June 1972. The American public was then in a more punitive mood than six years earlier when the abolitionist sentiment had been at its peak. During these six years, the proportion of those demanding harsher treatment of criminals grew from 48 to 66 percent[65] and of those favoring capital punishment, from 42 to 50.[66] However, with respect to the death penalty, this was a wavering change: the proportion of retentionists, which jumped from 42 to 51 percent of the total population between 1966 and 1969, stopped growing and was only slightly oscillating through March 1972 (to then rapidly increase again).[67] Thus, the society was confused, hesitant, and divided, and its wavering and divisions found a clear reflection in the cleavage among the *Furman* Justices and in their inability to determine the per se validity of capital punishment.

The following four years—that is, the years preceding pronouncement of *Gregg* in July 1976—brought about a steep increase in punitive attitudes. The view that courts were not harsh enough with criminals, accepted by 66 percent of the total population in 1972, was approved by 81 percent in 1976.[68] The proportion of those favoring the death penalty for murder grew from 53 to 66 percent.[69] Advocates of mandatory death sentences also increased,[70] as did those who would have opted for capital punishment even if it were ineffective in preventing crime.[71] This punitive mood was more and more forcefully expressed by a growing number of vocal individuals and of groups organized to reinforce the punitive attitude of the general public and to pressure policymakers, lawmakers, and the system of criminal justice. The zeal with which the state and federal lawmakers rushed to patch the capital laws in the wake of *Furman* should be perceived as an outcome of this pressure.

The Court responded to this sweeping change in general attitudes by pronouncing *Gregg* and the follow-up decisions. This response has been analyzed earlier. Only two Justices, Marshall and Brennan, appeared immune to the new, punitive mood and persisted in their struggle for total abolition. All others declared the constitutional validity of the death penalty, five of them also supporting the death sentence for policy reasons. In this manner, the causal chain of events came to its conclusion—from malfunctioning of criminal law; through the growth of crime, spreading anger and fear, and increase of punitive attitudes; to the decisions of the Supreme Court, which validated capital punishment, paved the way for return of executions, and dashed the hopes of the abolitionists. Today, we are left with one question: how lasting is the new validity of the death penalty?

CHAPTER 8

FUTURE DEVELOPMENTS

Predictions are risky, especially predictions on a social issue as emotional and controversial as the subject of this book. Still, the preceding considerations provide room for some reasonably safe guessing. The social forces responsible for what has happened to the death penalty under the American law were identified in earlier chapters, and the future operation of these forces can be, to a degree, anticipated. Consequently, a cautious, conditional conjecture on the future of the death penalty itself seems feasible.

The previous development of capital laws in America was presented here as an outcome of a clash between two opposing forces. One of these forces has been the cultural progress and gradual achievement of the level of development that this society enjoys—a force precipitating the tendency toward decreasing harshness of criminal penalties and, in particular, toward the abolition of capital punishment. This is a force that will stay with us. To be sure, a disaster, such as a major war, can remove this force by pushing us centuries back; however, it seems reasonable to assume that no such cataclysm will occur and that this society does not face cultural decline in any predictable future.

The second force consists in a malfunctioning of criminal justice. We saw how, by producing growth of crime, the malfunctioning has hindered the tendency toward decreasing harshness.

The malfunctioning constitutes one of those counteracting influences that have, in various progressing societies, limited the operation of the tendency.[1] In contrast with the first of the two forces under discussion—the high level of cultural development—the malfunctioning of criminal justice may be eliminated; it is a peculiar historical coincidence rather than a necessarily lasting characteristic of our social system. Since malfunctioning of criminal justice has had a decisive impact on the development of death penalty laws, the future of the penalty in this country seems largely dependent on whether the malfunctioning will continue or will be removed. In other terms, the future depends on whether this society decides to rectify the system of criminal justice and in this way to control crime.

The question of how criminal justice can be rectified has already been discussed. In a society on this country's level of development, criminal law should operate primarily as an implement of moral education of the society at large, though this does not preclude criminal law's playing other auxiliary roles such as general and individual deterrence. The main prerequisites for the educative function have also been spelled out earlier: criminal punishments must be reasonably certain and just. Neither prerequisite is being met in America today. Hence, practical implications of the earlier chapters seem clear: uncertainty and injustice are to be eliminated.

How do we eliminate the uncertainty and injustice? Again, in the light of the previous comments, the answer seems obvious. Those who run the system of criminal justice must operate under an enforceable obligation to comply with the law. In particular, the police should be (not only formally) duty bound to enforce criminal law with respect to every criminal offense they learn of, provided, of course, that the perpetrator can be located and that the offense seems provable. If the suspect's guilt can be expected to be proved in court, the prosecutor should be duty bound to charge him with the crime committed. And, especially, the judges must be duty bound to impose the prescribed punishment for every crime proved to have been committed. This would spell the end to both arbitrary nonenforcement and arbitrariness in determining severity of the penalties imposed—and, in particular, an end to plea bargaining, an embarrassing procedure accepted by no other civilized society. There is nothing new in at least some of these suggestions. What is new is the emphasis on their specific reason—the educative effects of their implementation rather than the often stressed ultimate value of retribution or teleology of deterrence.

These recommendations mean not an assult on discretion but only on perversions of discretion. A reasonable degree of discretion, especially in judicial sentencing, is unavoidable. This is so because the sentencing discretion, which may generate injustice, also constitutes a prerequisite for justice. In a civilized society, to be just, punishment must fit the amount of guilt, and since for any kind of crime this amount varies from case to case, there must be some room left for discretionary gradation of punitive measures. The room can be provided only by sentencing alternatives and, in particular, sentencing ranges.[2] Thus, what should be expected from criminal courts amounts to discretion without capriciousness; the measure of punishment should never cross the statutory boundaries prescribed for the crime committed, and within these boundaries, the measure should match, as well as feasible, the degree of guilt of the defendant.

The recommended remedies sound simple. But are they not, in fact, simplistic rather than simple, and is it not naïve to expect that they may be introduced at all? An emerging air of despair about crime can be traced around, in particular among scholars, journalists, and lawyers—a feeling that the problem is not only getting out of control but also cannot be effectively handled and, especially, that no effective legal reform is feasible. If this belief is correct, the remedies recommended here cannot be implemented effectively, and a number of reasons may be used to support this belief and this skeptical conclusion.

Indeed, it would be naïve to overlook how difficult the process of amending the system might be. First, the suddenly introduced strict enforcement would make costs of administration of justice prohibitive. Limiting discretion and, especially, removing negotiated pleas would, for want of a vast investment of financial and human resources, "break down administration of criminal justice in any state of the Union."[3] Furthermore, because of the tradition of feeble enforcement, our criminal laws are largely overshot—they prohibit an excessively broad range of behavior with the assumption that the feebleness of enforcement would strike the balance. Thus, the sudden introduction of the rigorous enforcement might result in an impossible proportion of us ending up in confinement.[4] Moreover, the exercise of wide discretion is a traditional privilege of those who run the system of criminal justice. Since they, especially the judges, wield considerable political clout, how can we persuade them to abandon much of their privilege? In particular, how can we persuade judges, prosecutors, and defense attorneys to abandon plea bargaining despite their well-established habits?[5] And there are two further, more general, arguments. One of them is historical; what has been proposed here implies a major legal change, whereas, traditionally, only piecemeal, cautiously empirical reforms have been characteristic of the development of American law. The other argument deals with the political process. Under this country's constitutional system, any major reform of criminal justice requires wide consensus. However, in a pluralistic society such as ours, the functioning of criminal justice is an area in which evaluations of various groups openly clash, and the clashes preclude the emergence of consensus needed for reform.

These are important arguments, but their weight should not be overstated. To be sure, criminal justice constitutes a complex system of interdependent behavior; that is why any significant change in some of its components may imperil the operation of others. This, however, implies only the need for further, adaptive changes in the other components affected, and in this case, a number of such adaptations would have to follow the proposed reform. In particular, there would be among them an extensive cutting-down of the overshot lists of crimes on the law books, a reduction in harshness of the prescribed sanctions, replacement of confinement by milder penalties—especially fines—for various kinds of *mala prohibita*, and a far-reaching simplification of procedure, whose complexity, expensiveness, and slowness are unparalleled by that of any other open society. These changes would reduce the work load and expenditure, and by decriminalizing some offenses and treating others more leniently, they would help avoid the excessive harshness.

It is true that all this means a reform of major proportions. (I have made a more detailed description of the reform elsewhere.[6]) Implementing the reform would be complex and difficult[7] and would demand generating much political will. However, there seems to be no other way to effectively deal with the crime problem, and an effective policy is badly needed and increasingly demanded. The demand, precipitated by the spreading fear of and anger about crime, finds an expression in the changing public and professional opinion of the past fifteen years. And this changing mood, if well informed and organized, may, even in a pluralist society and despite some special interests, produce a degree of consensus sufficient for an effective reform of criminal justice.

To be sure, this changing mood does not change exactly in the optimal direction stipulated here. Anger, fear, and the resulting hatred of the wrongdoer do not necessarily stimulate the idea of the general moral education; they rather arouse the wish to deter strongly or to take revenge. Consequently, they spur requests for severe, rather than merely certain and just, punishments and, especially, for capital punishment—the severity increases deterrence and makes revenge sweeter.

From the standpoint of the effectiveness of criminal justice, this widely demanded severity is harmless, and so are, in particular, capital convictions and executions for a heinous crime. They are harmless for two reasons: first, and obviously so, they do not contribute to uncertainty of punishments, and second, by being widely demanded, they are not perceived as unjust. On the other hand, they do not seem useful either. First, they do not enhance punitive certainty. Furthermore, they are not a prerequisite for justice. Our feeling of justice with respect to severity of punishments is, as has been shown earlier, vague. That is why the majority of us—those who opt against abolition—may prefer capital conviction but would accept also genuine life imprisonment as a reasonably just penalty for even the worst cases of the gravest crime. In this sense, the greater harshness of criminal penalties, and especially the new validity and return of executions in the wake of *Gregg*, are neither harmful nor useful for the effective operation of criminal justice; they are simply irrelevant.

In this manner the angry and fearful reaction against the pervasiveness of crime in America has addressed the irrelevant themes of punitive harshness and capital punishment rather than the more important issues of the certainty and justice. There is nothing unusual about this blunder. With respect to any major social problem where facts are unclear and evaluations differ, the society undergoes a slowly proceeding and wavering "referendum" where conflicting solutions are proposed and contested, and some of them tried. These solutions are often imperfect, and the resort to punitive harshness and the death penalty in America is simply an instance of a misdirected and thus imperfect solution for a major problem. In many societies, in the course of the ongoing "referendum," through trial, error, and exchange of information and ideas, the imperfect solutions of various social problems are eventually rectified. The chance of rectification is highest in open and well-educated societies, where ideas abound and information is easily accumulated, where the flow of ideas and information is never arrested, and where the general public, illuminated by this flow, has a say in the choice of policies. For these reasons there is a good chance that this society will eventually find out why crime rates continue to be exorbitant despite the return of executions and that it will rectify its response to the crime problem by addressing the critical issues of punitive certainty and punitive justice. These chances are further enhanced by the fact that both issues have been stressed in America often and at length (even though none of them has been perceived as the main policy issue or recommended for the sake of moral learning). In particular, the claim that criminal punishments be just, however deficiently implemented, has always been considered an obvious demand; and the value of punitive certainty, although never adhered to by the American courts, has been, since Bentham and Beccaria, ever present in the Anglo-American thinking on criminal justice.

Granted that the reform of criminal justice stipulated here occurs, what is the future of the death penalty? The reform will bring us closer to the state where a just punishment follows every crime committed. This will, in turn, bring, through the process of persuasive instrumental learning, a sweeping decline in criminal behavior. With crime under control, the anger and the fear of crime that pervade this society will disappear. The anger and fear absent, the tendency toward declining harshness of criminal punishments, then unopposed, will start working again. This cannot but bring about a new growth of the abolitionist sentiment, and eventually, the day of Justices Marshall and Brennan should come, even though not necessarily through the action of the Supreme Court.

Great social ideas can be implemented when congenial social conditions prevail, in particular, when a society reaches the level of development where such ideas can function. Otherwise, they remain fantasies or noble utopias. For instance, the idea of parliamentary democracy, when pronounced in primitive societies, is utopian; so were the Stoic ethical ideals of the Hellenistic decline,[8] and so were, whenever claimed, demands of punitive mildness in Germanic tribes of the Middle Ages. But in America, the idea of leniency and, especially, of the abolition of the death penalty is not of that brand. The progress already made by this society—the civilization of America—makes the idealism of Justices Marshall and Brennan clearly practicable and makes of both of them proponents of a realistic legal change rather than utopians in the Stoic style.

NOTES

INTRODUCTION; and 1. FURMAN v. GEORGIA

1. In Michigan, the death penalty was retained for treason, and in Rhode Island, for murder committed by an inmate while serving a life sentence.

2. Maine abolished the death penalty in 1876, restored it in 1883, and reabolished it in 1887 (cf. note 50 to chapter 6, *infra*).

3. Cf. chapter 6, text to note 46, *infra*.

4. 408 U.S. 238 (1972).

5. Words of Chief Justice Warren that Justices Brennan and Marshall quote approvingly in *Furman*, pp. 269–70, 327, and 329.

6. Justice Marshall in *Furman*, p. 329. (Cf. also Trop v. Dulles, 356 U.S. 86, 100–1 [1958]; Weems v. United States, 217 U.S. 349, 373 [1910.]

7. *Furman*, p. 270.

8. *Ibid.*, pp. 271–73 and 286–91.

9. *Ibid.*, pp. 274–77 and 291–95.

10. *Ibid.*, p. 279.

11. The degrading character of capital punishment finds, in Justice Brennan's view, an additional corroboration. One can assume that a degrading penalty would be rejected by the society. The progressive decline in executions and their current rarity demonstrate that capital punishment has been widely rejected. Thus, its rejection corroborates its degrading character (*Furman*, pp. 277 and 299–300). This is, however, an invalid point. True, if capital punishment were clearly degrading, the majority of Americans would probably opt against it. But the fact that the majority of Americans opt against it—assuming that they, indeed, do—does not necessarily imply that it is degrading. They may opt against it because of its extreme harshness (i.e., "cruelty" in the usual sense of the term), its bad side effects, the aesthetic aversion it arouses, or another reason.

12. *Furman*, pp. 332–33.

13. I am introducing the expression "teleologically excessive" to make a

distinction between two kinds of excessiveness. An "excessive penalty" may mean a punishment unjustly severe for the crime committed (as in Weems v. United States, 217 U.S. 349 [1910]) or unnecessarily severe for achievement of intended goals. Justice Marshall deals, somewhat indiscriminately, with both kinds. However, he uses only the latter—the teleological excessiveness of capital punishment—as an argument for the abolition.

14. *Furman*, pp. 331–32, 342, 359.

15. *Ibid.*, pp. 342–59; the quotation is from p. 359.

16. *Ibid.*, pp. 360–69.

17. While some of these arguments sound strong, others arouse doubts. The judicial interpreter of a statutory (and constitutional) norm is bound, when defining nontechnical expressions of the norm, by their ordinary meaning. "Cruel" is, basically, a nontechnical term. When referred to punishments, it means, in the ordinary language, a penalty that arouses, because of its extreme harshness, the feeling of moral outrage. Even though this ordinary meaning underlies their arguments, the abolitionist Justices do not adhere consistently to it. This is particularly true of Justice Brennan's identification of a punishment's cruelty with its degrading, humiliating character. An intentionally and gravely humiliating penalty, such as pillorying a culprit or his public ridicule at execution, is, of course, always cruel. However, in today's civilized societies, cruelty of criminal punishment, that is, its extreme harshness, whenever it occurs, does not necessarily imply the humiliation; indeed, humiliation is most often absent (unless we treat any criminal punishment as degrading and humiliating). Justice Brennan also disregards the ordinary meaning of the common terms by claiming that arbitrariness of punishment is degrading and, therefore, cruel. To be sure, arbitrariness can be both degrading and cruel if it occurs for intentionally categorical reasons—for instance, if the court tells the convict that he would not have been convicted but for being black or poor or deaf. However, the arbitrariness claimed by Justice Brennan is, apparently, not intended by judges or juries. It is rather their broad and unstructured discretionary powers that make the judges and juries largely unable to adhere to the principle "Treat like cases alike." (If this inadherence runs against any constitutional provisions, it is rather against the Equal Protection or Due Process Clauses than against the Eighth Amendment.)

Also Justice Marshall's understanding of "cruelty" disregards the ordinary meaning of the term. In Justice Marshall's words, purposeless penalties or penalties unnecessarily severe to achieve intended aims are cruel and thus "unconstitutional even though popular sentiment may favor them" (*Furman* p. 331). This implies cruelty of even a mild punishment if the punishment is ineffective or if a still milder sanction would do. Under this construction, a $10 fine would be cruel if enacted with the exclusive purpose to deter, and if it does not deter at all or if $1 would deter equally effectively. Justice Marshall lists Weems v. United States (217 U.S. 349 [1910]) and Robinson v. California (370 U.S. 660 [1972]) among the decisions that had earlier accepted this understanding of "cruelty" (*Furman*, pp. 328 and 331–32). Needless to say, this understanding contrasts with the ordinary meaning of the term "cruel"; in plain English, even a useless or teleologically excessive penalty is not cruel if it does not arouse any moral indignation. Moreover, this understanding may hardly be derived from the decisions to which Justice Marshall refers. True, *Weems* did prohibit excessive penalties, but there an "excessive penalty" meant a sanction abhorrently severe for the crime committed, and not a sanction unnecessarily severe for achievement of intended aims (cf. note 13, *supra*); and the *Robinson* majority struck down, as abhorrent, any penalty imposed on anyone who had not committed an *actus reus*, but they did not refer at all to excessive or purposeless penalties.

18. Some commentators lay stronger stress on the difference between the stand of the two abolitionist Justices. (Cf., e.g., Donnelly, "Theory of Justice," p. 1109.) To be sure, the difference is there. In particular, in contrast with Justice Marshall, Justice Brennan does not directly reduce the cruelty of punishment to the society's moral outrage. However, he does so indirectly. He identifies cruelty with infringement of human dignity; whether a penalty violates the dignity eventually depends, in his opinion, upon the society's changing moral views. (See on this his approving references to *Weems* in *Furman*, pp. 269–70, esp. p. 270, n. 10.)

19. According to the Fifth Amendment, no one "shall be held to answer for a capital . . . crime, unless on a presentment or indictment of a Grand Jury . . ., nor shall any person . . . be twice put in jeopardy of life;" and both the Fifth and Fourteenth Amendement require that no person shall be deprived "of life . . . without due process of law." Moreover, the First Congress introduced, almost simultaneously with the Eighth Amendment, death penalty for a number of crimes (in the first Criminal Act of 1790, C. 9, 1 Stat. 112).

20. Cf. Chief Justice Burger in *Furman*, p. 380, and Justice Powell, *ibid.*, pp. 418–20.

21. Justice Powell in *Furman*, p. 417, Cf. also Justice Powell, *ibid.*, pp. 421–28; Chief Justice Burger, *ibid.*, pp. 380–81, 399–400; Justice Blackmun, *ibid.*, pp. 407–9.

22. In Wilkerson v. Utah, 99 U.S. 130, 134–35 (1879).

23. In McGautha v. California, 402 U.S. 183 (1971), cf., in particular, words of Justice Black, p. 226.

24. Chief Justice Burger in *Furman*, p. 383. Cf. also his words, *ibid.*, pp. 403–5; Justice Blackmun, *ibid.*, pp. 410–11, 413; Justice Powell, *ibid.*, pp. 417–18, 431–33, 461–62; Justice Rehnquist, *ibid.*, p. 466.

25. Justice Powell, *ibid.*, p. 462.

26. Words of Justice Frankfurter quoted by Justice Powell, *ibid.*, p. 433.

27. Cf. Justice Powell, *ibid.*, pp. 417–18, 461–62; Justice Rehnquist, *ibid.*, pp. 469–70.

28. Justice Powell, *ibid.*, p. 458. Cf. also Justice Powell, *ibid.*, pp. 417–18, 431–33; Chief Justice Burger, *ibid.*, pp. 384, 405; Justice Rehnquist, *ibid.*, pp. 467–69.

29. Cf. *ibid.*, pp. 451–59.
30. *Furman*, p. 375.
31. *Ibid.*, pp. 406–7.
32. *Ibid.*, pp. 249–57.
33. *Ibid.*, p. 309. In this new understanding not just the death penalty itself but the process of its imposition is perceived as cruel (cf. Radin, "Cruel Punishment," p. 1143.)
34. *Ibid.*, pp. 310–14; the quotation comes from p. 313.
35. *Ibid.*, p. 316. This idea had been powerfully expressed, a few years earlier, by Goldberg and Dershowitz ("Declaring Death Penalty Unconstitutional," p. 1773).
36. Cf. Friedman, *History of American Law*, p. 252.
37. Cf. chapter 7, text to notes 9–31, *infra*.
38. In Justice Powell's words, "[t]he same . . . argument could be made with equal force and logic with respect to those sentenced to prison terms" (*Furman*, p. 447).
39. However, of course, bargaining may prevent a court from inflicting the death penalty.
40. In McGautha v. California, 402 U.S. 183 (1970).
41. The reversal was not explicit: *McGautha* has never been overruled, neither in *Furman* nor in Gregg v. Georgia (428 U.S. 153, 195–96 note 47 [1976]), where the Stewart plurality only distinguished *McGautha* as a Fourteenth Amendment case from *Gregg* (and *Furman*) as Eighth Amendment cases. The distinction is dubious, however. Arbitrariness of the jury runs more against Equal Protection and Due Process clauses than against the Eighth Amendment (cf. note 17, *supra*).

2. FURMAN TO GREGG

1. *Furman*, pp. 400–1.
2. Riedel, "Discrimination in Imposition of Death Penalty," p. 261 and p. 261 note 3.
3. Louisiana Rev. Stat. Ann., Para. 14:30.
4. Georgia Code Ann., Para. 26–3102.
5. 428 U.S. 153 (1976).
6. Proffitt v. Florida, 428 U.S. 242 (1976); Jurek v. Texas, 428 U.S. 262 (1976); Woodson v. North Carolina, 428 U.S. 280 (1976); Roberts v. Louisiana, 428 U.S. 325 (1976).
7. In *Gregg*, p. 169.
8. In Woodson v. North Carolina, 428 U.S. 280, 285–305 (1976). Here, however, the Court refused to answer the question whether a mandatory death penalty statute would be unconstitutional if "limited to an extremely narrow category of homicide, such as murder by a prisoner serving a life sentence, defined in large part in terms of the character or record of the offender" (*ibid.*, p. 287, note 7). Cf. also *ibid.*, pp. 292–93, note 25; Roberts v. Louisiana, 428

U.S. 325, 334 note 9 (1976); Harry Roberts v. Louisiana, 431 U.S. 633, 634–35 (1977); Lockett v. Ohio, 438 U.S. 586, 605 note 11 (1978). For a critical examination of this stand of the Court, see Frankel, "Constitutionality of Mandatory Death Penalty," p. 636.

9. *Gregg*, p. 184; cf. also p. 183.

10. *Ibid.*, pp. 179–80.

11. *Ibid.*, p. 182.

12. Cf. chapter 1, text to notes 9, 33 and 34, *supra*.

13. *Gregg*, p. 184, note 30.

14. *Ibid.*, p. 183 (quoted after Justice Stewart's concurring opinion in *Furman*).

15. *Ibid.*, p. 185.

16. *Ibid.*, p. 185–86.

17. Jurek v. Texas, 428 U.S. 262, 279 (1976).

18. Roberts v. Louisiana, 428 U.S. 325, 354 (1976).

19. *Ibid.*

20. P. 312.

21. Roberts v. Louisiana, 428 U.S. 325, 355 (1976).

22. Harry Roberts v. Louisiana, 431 U.S. 633 (1977).

23. *Ibid.*

24. In Lockett v. Ohio, 438 U.S. 586 (1978). This was a case where the defendant "did not kill anybody, did not try to kill anybody, did not suggest that anybody be killed, and did not know anybody would be killed" (Black, "Death Penalty Now," pp. 429–30). Cf. also Justice O'Connor's subsequent refusal to preclude capital punishment for felony murder, in her dissent from Enmund v. Oklahoma, 102 S.Ct.869 (1982).

3. LEGAL CHANGE

1. This was only a basic proclamation; it did not entirely preclude exceptions (cf. chapter 2, note 8, *supra*).

2. *Gregg*, pp. 206–7.

3. The mandatory death penalty was, on the eve of *Furman*, unknown for all practical purposes, but it stayed for some crimes, especially for treason, on the law books of more than a dozen jurisdictions; cf. Bedau, *Death Penalty in America*, (Anchor Books), 46–52.

4. For a more extensive criticism of plea bargaining, see chapter 6, text to notes 20–31, *infra*.

5. Black, *Capital Punishment*, p. 43; cf. also Note: "New Death Penalty Statutes," pp. 1712–19.

6. Cf., e.g., van den Haag, *Punishing Criminals*, p. 162; Zimring, O'Malley, and Eigen, "Going Price of Criminal Homicide," p. 277. The very threat of execution, by providing defendants with a particularly strong motivation to negotiate, pushes the proportion upward—see, in particular, Brady v. United States, 397 U.S. 742 (1970), Parker v. North Carolina, 397 U.S. 790 (1970),

North Carolina v. Alford, 400 U.S. 25 (1970). On the other hand, however, capital crimes arouse, more often than lesser offenses, high publicity and widespread anger, and whenever this happens, it may be difficult for the prosecution to avoid the full-fledged trial.

7. The term *guilt* has a number of meanings. In this context, it denotes the society's feeling of blameworthiness of a defendant's criminal act.

8. This is a widespread stand, however difficult its explanation might be; on the explanatory difficulties, cf., e.g., Schulhofer, "Harm and Punishment," p. 1497.

9. On the high degree of consensus about the relative gravity of crimes, cf, e.g., Rossi, Waite, Bose, and Berk, "Seriousness of Crimes," p. 224; Figlio, "Seriousness of Offenses," p. 189.

10. This wording of the precept comes from Radbruch, *Rechtsphilosophie*, p. 46.

11. This explains the outcome of a 1977 public opinion survey. A random sample of adults in the United States was asked: "In general, do you feel that judges should: be required to give the same sentence for a particular crime regardless of the circumstances of the case; have limited power to make sentences 'tougher' or 'lighter' depending on the circumstances of the case?" Only 11 percent of respondents opted for mandatory sentences, 58 percent favoring limited, and 28 percent, great judicial discretionary power (*Sourcebook of Criminal Justice Statistics 1979*, 1980, p. 287, table 2.49).

12. Which, however, is not the case in the United States.

13. See chapter 2, note 24, *supra*.

14. Roberts v. Louisiana, 428 U.S. 325, 339–40 (1976).

15. Proffitt v. Florida, 428 U.S. 242, 245 (1976).

16. *Gregg*, pp. 158–60.

17. Jurek v. Texas, 428 U.S. 262, 266–67 (1976).

18. The impossibility of effectively controlling discretion in capital cases had been claimed before *Furman*. For instance, in McGautha v. California, 402 U.S. 183 (1971), the Court insisted that "[t]o identify before the fact those characteristics of criminal homicides and their perpetrators which call for the death penalty, and to express these characteristics in language which can be fairly understood and applied by the sentencing authority, appear to be tasks which are beyond present human ability" (p. 204). For explanation of this stand, the Court referred to the Report of the Royal Commission on Capital Punishment: "No formula is possible that would provide a reasonable criterion for the infinite variety of circumstances that may affect the gravity of the crime of murder" (*ibid.*, p. 205). There may be some validity to this claim, but "the infinite variety of circumstances" is not the main reason why discretion in capital cases cannot be controlled. Even if we were able to invent an elaborate formula suggesting, in detail, all the relevant circumstances that should be taken into account, the law would have to refer to the degree of guilt and dominant feeling of justice as the ultimate criteria, and the vagueness of these criteria cannot but result in arbitrary decisions in the majority of capital dispositions.

19. Ga. Stat. Ann., Para. 26–1101 (c) (1972).

20. Ga. Stat. Ann., Para. 27–2534.1 (b) (Supp. 1976).

21. Ga. Stat. Ann., Para. 27–2534.1 (b) (7) (Supp. 1976). On a later, restrictive interpretation of this norm by the Supreme Court, see Godfrey v. Georgia, 100 S. Ct. 1759 (1980).

22. Fla. Stat. Ann., Para. 921.141 (5) (h) (Supp. 1976–77).

23. Fla. Stat. Ann., Para. 921.141 (3) (Supp. 1976–77).

24. Tex. Code Crim. Pro., Art. 37.071 (b) (2), (c), and (d) (1).

25. If literally interpreted, the norm seems to be an implement of individual prevention but not of civilized justice: "People are . . . to live or die, in Texas, on a jury's *guess* as to their *future* conduct" (Black, *Capital Punishment*, p. 62). The norm demands a prediction that a jury will rarely be able to make. And it claims, in a manner dangerously close to self-contradiction, that a "probability" be established "beyond reasonable doubt" (cf. Black, *ibid.*, p. 63, and "Due Process for Death," pp. 1, 4–5.

26. In Jurek v. Texas, 428 U.S. 262, 272–74 (1976).

27. *Woodson*, p. 304.

28. *Lockett*, p. 604. This view has been strongly reaffirmed in Eddings v. Oklahoma, 102 S.Ct.869 (1982).

29. Cf. *Gregg*, pp. 188–92.

30. ALI, Model Penal Code, Para. 201.6, Comment 5, p. 75 (Tent. Draft No. 9, 1959), quoted in *Gregg*, p. 191. On the value of bifurcated proceedings, see Meltsner, *Cruel and Unusual*, pp. 68–69.

31. Cf., e.g., the law of Georgia (Ga. Stat. Ann., Para. 27–2537, Supp. 1976), Florida (Fla. Stat. Ann., Para. 921.141/4, Supp. 1976–77), and Texas (Tex. Code Crim. Proc. Art. 37.071 f, Supp. 1975–76). In 1976, the Court made the automatic review a prerequisite for the validity of capital punishment (Roberts v. Louisiana, 428 U.S. 325, 335–36 [1976]).

32. On its frequently improper implementation, see, e.g., Black, "Due Process for Death," pp. 8 and 14–15; Dix, "Administration of Texas Death Penalty Statutes," pp. 1343, 1403–7, 1409–10, 1412–13; Dix, "Appellate Review of Decision," p. 97.

33. This change has also another, broader implication: it seems to be an important step (and stimulus) toward the increasingly expanding appellate review of sentences in general.

34. 433 U.S 584 (1977).

35. Cf. chapter 1, note 13, *supra*.

36. Cf., in particular, Browning, "New Death Penalty Statutes," pp. 651, 684; Dix, "Administration of Texas Death Penalty Statutes," pp. 1343, 1403–7, 1409–10, 1412–13; Dix, "Appellate Review of Decision," pp. 144–58; Riedel, "Discrimination in Imposition of Death Penalty," p. 268 ff; Baldus, Pulaski, Woodworth, and Kyle, "Identifying Comparatively Excessive Sentences of Death," pp. 18–21; Arkin, Note: "Discrimination and Arbitrariness," pp. 98–100; Pierce, "Arbitrariness and Discrimination," p. 563.

p   37. Justice White in *Lockett*, p. 622.

38. *Furman*, p. 403.

4. CRIMINAL PUNISHMENT

1. The evolutionary perspective in humanities and, especially, in what then constituted social sciences was dominant in much of the 1800s. In the first half of our century, however, this perspective all but disappeared from both America and Europe; it was replaced, among others, by the idiographic stand of historians, by the intuitive essentialism of phenomenologists, and above all, by the positivist minimalism of all those too cautious to speculate about general dynamics of development. In consequence, as one leading philosopher complained, they did "engage in sociography instead of sociology, dialectography instead of a general theory of language, philological textual criticism instead of a comprehensive interpretation of literary currents, etc." (Kotarbiński, *Gnosiology*, p. 494). Since the 1950s the mood has changed. We have experienced a revival of evolutionary thinking, old and new, in a variety of fields. We experience it in particular in the disciplines that deal with the past and the future of human society.

2. This is one important tenet of the Marxists: "The mode of production . . . conditions the social, political and intellectual life process . . . [in particular] the hand-mill gives you a society with the feudal lord; the steam-mill gives you a society with the industrial capitalist" (Marx, "Critique of Political Economy," p. 363). Economic explanation has been claimed also by a number of cultural anthropologists, old and new: "We view technology as the wellspring of the changes that have made for evolutionary progress" (Goldschmidt, *Man's Way*, p. 114).

3. Goldschmidt, *Man's Way*, p. 119.

4. The majority of these and similar explanations concentrate only on the evolution of human society. Often, however, social evolution is perceived as a component of a more general development such as evolution of all living matter or even of cosmic evolution. Then the forces believed to produce this all-embracing development are also used as at least a partial explanation for its social component. These forces include genetic chance and environmental necessity as sociobiological conditions of cultural change, Bergsonian "élan vital" stimulating the "creative evolution" of living organisms, and Marxist "struggle of opposites"—the universal mainspring of "development of nature, human society and thought" (Engels, *Anti-Dühring*, p. 158).

5. The general idea of declining harshness of criminal sanctions was expressed, at the beginning of the century, by Petrażycki and Durkheim. Petrażycki treated the idea as part of a broader notion of the tendency to diminish motivational pressure (both in terms of rewards and punishments) in the course of improvement of human character (Petrażycki, *Teoriia prava*, pp. 754–56; see also Lande, "Sociology of Petrażycki," p. 31; and Podgórecki, "Unrecognized Father," pp. 193–94). Durkheim claimed that extreme severity of criminal law declines with increasing division of labor and differentiation of society, provided that governmental power becomes decentralized (Durkheim, "Two Laws of Penal Evolution," pp. 153–80; for a recent criticism of

Durkheim's claim, see Spitzer, "Punishment and Social Organization," pp. 614–37).

6. Such prophecies have been made in the past, in particular by the Marxists, who anticipated disappearance of socially harmful behavior in a classless society and, subsequently, disappearance of criminal law (Cf., e.g., Engels, *Condition of the Working Class*, pp. 145–49, 227, 242–43; Engels, *Anti-Dühring*, pp. 308–9; see also Lenin, *State and Revolution*, p. 75). Also Petrażycki's moral evolutionism anticipates eventual abolition of criminal sanctions. From the standpoint of this book, a similar view may seem reasonable: an everlasting trend toward disappearance of the harshest of the penalties actually known may eventually lead to removal of all punishments. This takes too much for granted, however, in terms of predictable, linear, everlasting progress.

7. On the idea of increasing social demands, see Petrażycki, *Teoriia prava*, pp. 754–55; Lande, "Sociology of Petrażycki," pp. 29–30; Podgórecki, "Unrecognized Father," p. 193; Podgórecki, *Law and Society*, pp. 217–18.

8. For the estimated size of the citizen population in Athens, see Hammond, *History of Greece*, p. 528.

9. M. Rostovtzeff, *History of the Ancient World*, p. 204.

10. *Ibid.*, p. 287.

11. Thucydides, *History of the Peloponesian War*, Book II, XXXVII–XLI (Karl Popper's translation, as published in *Open Society*, pp. 186–87).

12. Emergence of criminal law is, in any primitive society, a somewhat vague occurrence, and so it was in Greece. Basically, by "criminal law" we understand norms prescribing penalties to be imposed by the state for commitment of public wrongs. This implies two conditions for the emergence of criminal law: some acts must become perceived as publicly harmful, and a state authority must exist strong enough to effectively punish those acts. Before these two conditions are met, there is only "private" response to wrongdoing— by the harmed individual or his kin or clan (even though the response is frequently supplemented by magic or religious sanctions). This private response varies among primitive societies. It often consists of blood feud, but once the feuds become too disruptive to the social peace, they may be replaced by composition—the primitive form of punitive damages. Emergence of criminal law follows under the two just mentioned conditions, but the emergence is rarely complete; the new public norms of criminal law contain various elements of private revenge or private restitution, as they did in Greece. For instance, under Draco, the criminal trial was already conducted by the state but at the complaint of the avenger. In the classical period, in cases of unintentional homicide, the victim's family could, for or without damages, release the killer from punishment (MacDowell, *Athenian Homicide Law*, pp. 120–23). Moreover, the victim of unintended or intentional homicide could release the killer from any liability if, before dying, the victim had expressed forgiveness (Harrison, *Law of Athens*, pp. 77–78).

13. Cf. Bonner and Smith, *Administration of Justice* 1:111–12; 3:2.

14. Cf. MacDowell, *Law in Classical Athens*, p. 43.

15. Hatzfield, *History of Ancient Greece*, p. 49. However, on the possibility that the distinction had been known earlier, see Freudenthal, "Antworten, Griechisch," p. 11.

16. Cf., e.g., Hatzfield, *ibid.*; Kurt Latte, "Beiträge zum Griechischen Strafrecht," pp. 294–95.

17. In particular, Lysias, Fragment 10 (Thalheim), Alkiphron II 38, 3, Diogenes Laert. I, 55.

18. *Plutarch's Lives.*

19. For a scrupulous comparative study of criminal penalties under primitive legal systems, see Diamond, *Primitive Law, passim.*

20. This is so, because Solon repealed the whole of Draco's code, except the homicide norms (cf. the following comment by Plutarch).

21. For a survey of these crimes, see Diamond, *Primitive Law*, pp. 92–103; the survey is largely relevant here, even though Diamond accepts economic change as the main indicator of social development.

22. Plutarch, *Solon* XVII.

23. Cf., e.g., MacDowell, *Law in Classical Athens*, pp. 125, 179.

24. *Ibid.*, p. 155.

25. *Ibid.*, pp. 148–49.

26. *Ibid.*, p. 135.

27. Both temple robbery and high treason were sanctioned not only by mandatory execution but also by additional penalties of no burial in Attica and confiscation of property (Harrison, *Law of Athens*, p. 59).

28. Even in the case of an intentional homicide there was, however, a way of avoiding execution; at the end of his first speech, the defendant was permitted to implicitly acknowledge his guilt by leaving the court and going into exile for the rest of his life. This choice "must often have been fiendishly hard, because it had to be made before the court gave its verdict. To be sure of avoiding death, a man had to go into exile without waiting to see whether the jury would acquit him. If he waited for the verdict at the end of the trial and then was found guilty, it was too late to go into exile . . . . The system contained a large element of gambling" (MacDowell, *Athenian Homicide Law*, p. 115). Indeed, this system seems to have been the first predecessor of plea bargaining, which pervades criminal justice in America today.

29. On changes in executions, see Irving Barkan, *Capital Punishment in Ancient Athens*, pp. 41–82.

30. Harrison, *Law of Athens*, p. 170.

31. MacDowell, *Law in Classical Athens*, p. 80; cf. also Harrison, *Law of Athens*, p. 169.

32. Harrison, *Law of Athens*, pp. 143–44, 173–75.

33. MacDowell, *Law in Classical Athens*, p. 43.

34. J. Walter Jones, *Law and Legal Theory*, p. 107.

35. The clean hands principle was expressed by the Romans as *Nemo turpitudinem suam allegans, audiatur*. On the educative influence of civil law, see chapter 5, note 22, *infra*.

36. Rostovtzeff, *History of the Ancient World*, 2:243.

37. Cf., e.g., A. H. M. Jones, *Criminal Courts of Roman Republic*, pp. 38–39.

38. Mommsen, *Römisches Strafrecht*, Leipzig: Duncker & Humbolt, 1899, pp. 4–5.

39. Table VIII, 2.

40. Table VIII, 23.

41. Table IX, 3.

42. Mommsen, *Römisches Strafrecht*, p. 668.

43. Table VIII, 1, 8a, 8b.

44. Mommsen, *Römisches Strafrecht*, pp. 631, 921–22.

45. Cf. Kunkel, *Roman Legal and Constitutional History*, p. 28; Jolowicz and Nicholas, *Study of Roman Law*, p. 167, note 6.

46. Table VIII, 14; moreover, a thief caught at night, and a thief caught in the daytime if he put up armed resistance, might be lawfully killed on the spot (Table VIII, 12, 13).

47. Table VIII, 12, 13.

48. Table VIII, 9.

49. Table VIII, 10.

50. Mommsen, *Römisches Strafrecht*, pp. 527, 761, 769.

51. Table III, 5, 6.

52. There certainly was some Greek influence on the law of XII Tables, but its extent has always been a controversial issue; for a brief review of the literature, see Jolowicz and Nicholas, *Study of Roman Law* pp. 111–13.

53. Table VIII, 24a.

54. Table VIII, 10.

55. Table VIII, 9.

56. The tradition comes from Cicero and his contemporaries. It has been widely accepted, among others by Mommsen, and challenged by some recent writers who either question the whole doctrine of *provocatio* (Kunkel, *Entwicklung des Römischen Kriminalverfahrens*) or believe that *provocatio* was introduced much later, possibly by the third *Lex Valeria* in 300 B.C.

57. By *Lex Poetelia*, enacted probably in 326 B.C. (Jolowicz and Nicholas, *Study of Roman Law*, pp. 189–90). This alleviation seems, however, to be an outcome, not only of the general tendency toward declining harshness of punitive measures, but also of the acute class struggle (*ibid.*, p. 87).

58. Jolowicz and Nicholas, *Study of Roman Law*, p. 274; Mommsen, *Römisches Strafrecht*, p. 773.

59. *Ibid.*, p. 770.

60. *Ibid.*

61. *Ibid.*, pp. 873–74.

62. *Ibid.*, p. 942; Jolowicz and Nicholas, *Study of Roman Law*, p. 307.

63. Mommsen, *Römisches Strafrecht*, pp. 644–45, 942.

64. *Ibid.*, p. 802; Jolowicz and Nicholas, *Study of Roman Law*, p. 272.

65. Cf. note 57, *supra*.
66. Jolowicz and Nicholas, *Study of Roman Law*, p. 274.
67. Strachan-Davidson, *Roman Criminal Law*, 1:165.
68. A. H. M. Jones, *Criminal Courts of Roman Republic*, p. 78.
69. Kunkel, *Roman Legal and Constitutional History*, p. 65.
70. Cf., e.g., Hippel, *Deutsches Strafrecht*, pp. 106, 117–18, 142–45, 189–93; Pollock and Maitland, *History of English Law*, 2:470 ff.
71. Enacted as *Des allerdurchleuchtigsten grossmachtigsten unüberwindlichsten Keyser Karls des fünfften und des heyligen Römischen Reichs peinlich gerichts ordnung*.
72. *Carolina* was either literally in force or replaced, in some of the German and Austrian lands, by criminal laws derived from it and thus similar to it.
73. These are instances of punishments selected from Articles 104–180 of the *Carolina*.
74. Cf., in general, Garçon, *Le droit pénal*; Esmain, *Histoire de la procédure criminelle*.
75. Stephen, *History of Criminal Law of England*, 1:466.
76. *Ibid.*, p. 468.
77. *Ibid.*, vol. 1, p. 476, 2:451; cf. also Radzinowicz, *History of English Criminal Law*, 1:209–27.
78. For instance, on the development of various corporal penalties for noncapital vagrancy and for begging, see Chambliss, "Sociological Analysis of Law of Vagrancy," pp. 67–77.
79. Cf. Radzinowicz, *History of English Criminal Law*, pp. 175–205.
80. Stephen, *History of Criminal Law of England*, pp. 297–99.
81. Strictly speaking, Beccaria advocated abolition of the death penalty except for those who, in times of social upheaval, "endanger the security of the nation" (Beccaria, *On Crimes and Punishments*, p. 46).
82. Salmonowicz, in his groundbreaking study *Criminal Law of Enlightened Despotism*, p. 46.
83. This and some other Austrian and Prussian data that follow come from Salmonowicz, *ibid.*
84. *Ibid.*, pp. 155–56. On the way in which the Declaration expressed the principle, see note 99, *infra*.
85. According to Para. 20 of the code, "The death penalty shall not be imposed, except for the crimes which must be dealt with by martial law."
86. Of the 1,171 criminals convicted to boat towing in 1784–89, 721 died before the 1790 abolition of the penalty (Salmonowicz, *Criminal Law of Enlightened Despotism* pp. 96–97).
87. In the years 1803–47, 1,183 defendants were sentenced to death for common crimes; 446 of them were executed, and 421 of these executions were for murder. (There were also, altogether, two executions for treason.) After 1848, the executions became even more rare. Cf. Salmonowicz, *Criminal Law of Enlightened Despotism* pp. 150–51, note 372.
88. The law of April 3, 1919.

89. According to Art. 85 of the Austrian Constitution, "The death penalty is abolished."

90. Hippel, *Deutsches Strafrecht*, pp. 273–74; Salmonowicz, *Criminal Law of Enlightened Despotism*, pp. 195–99.

91. Hippel, *Deutsches Strafrecht*, p. 274, note 4.

92. *Allgemeines Landrecht für die preussischen Staaten*. Norms of criminal law—altogether 1,577 paragraphs—constitute the twentieth chapter of the second part of the code.

93. Cf. Hälschner, *Das Preussische Strafrecht*, pp. 233–39.

94. *Das Preussische Strafgesetzbuch*, 1851.

95. The code was reenacted, first, in May 1870, as the *Strafgesetzbuch für den Norddeutschen Bund*, and then, one year later, as the *Strafgesetzbuch für das Deutsche Reich*.

96. In 1870, during the second parliamentary reading of the draft of the *Strafgesetzbuch für den Norddeutschen Bund* (see the preceding note), the Reichstag decided to abolish the death penalty, with 118 members voting for and 81 against the abolition. A few months later, during the third reading, the defeat of the abolitionists, 127 to 119, was engineered by Bismarck (Hippel, *Deutsches Strafrecht*, pp. 344–45).

97. *Das Geldstrafengesetz* of December 21, 1921.

98. *Das Jugendgerichtsgesetz* of February 17, 1923.

99. The Declaration expressed the principle in a particularly clear way: "No one can be punished except in virtue of a law established and promulgated prior to the offense" (Art. 8 *in fine*).

100. Art. 8 *in princ.*

101. *Code Pénal*, enacted February 12–20, 1810.

102. Cf. Sabatier, "Napoléon et les codes criminels," p. 905.

103. Merle and Vitu, *Traité de droit criminel*, p. 46.

104. Law of April 28, 1832. This was an extension of an earlier law, of June 25, 1824, which had introduced circumstances mitigating punishment, but for some crimes only.

105. Law of May 19, 1863 (which changed altogether sixty-five articles of the criminal code).

106. Law of May 27, 1885, added exile to their confinement; thus, thieves, on their first conviction, were to be deported for life to Guyana after release from prison.

107. According to the law of July 22, 1912, minors over thirteen were not only rehabilitated but also punished if mature enough to be held accountable; even then their age was, to a degree, a mitigating circumstance.

108. The support was indirect, because it was not just the leniency per se that was demanded by Marc Ancel, the main architect of the New Social Defense (cf., in particular, his *La défense sociale nouvelle*) and his numerous followers. Their main claim was to protect society from crime through criminal sanctions individually adapted to the personality of the offender and, thus,

facilitating his resocialization whenever feasible. Since great harshness hardly ever helps resocializing anyone, the New Social Defense has had an indirect moderating influence on the severity of criminal sanctions.

109. By the *Ordonnance* of February 2, 1945 (subsequently amended in 1951 and 1958).

110. In 1958, by Articles 738–47 of the Code of Criminal Procedure.

111. Cf. Bouzat and Pinatel, *Traité de droit pénal*, pp. 819–20, 828.

112. Law of November 23, 1950.

113. By the *Ordonnance* of June 4, 1960 (enacted in the rather violent period of decolonization).

114. By law of April 13, 1954.

115. That is all except the political crimes adjudicated, since 1963, by the *Cour de sûreté de l'Etat*.

116. Cf. Merle and Vitu, *Traité de droit criminal*, p. 516; and Stefani and Lavasseur, *Droit pénal général*, p. 322, note 3.

117. Cf. chapter 4, text to note 75, *supra*.

118. Blackstone's *Commentaries on the Laws of England*, vol. IV, comm. 18.

119. Radzinowicz, *History of English Criminal Law*, p. 4.

120. Which was, in fact, less severe than a general norm sanctioning a single crime of any forgery by death. (The quotation comes from Stephen, *History of Criminal Law of England*, p. 470.)

121. Radzinowicz, *History of English Criminal Law*, pp. 10–11, 60–66.

122. Stephen, *History of Criminal Law of England*, p. 485.

123. Words of Sir Archibald Macdonald, quoted after Radzinowicz, *History of English Criminal Law*, p. 343.

124. Cf. Radzinowicz, *ibid.*, pp. 91–93.

125. *Ibid.*, pp. 83–91.

126. *Ibid.*, pp. 93–97, 144–45.

127. *Ibid.*, p. 97.

128. *Ibid.*, pp. 107–37.

129. Cf. Stephen, *History of Criminal Law of England*, pp. 469–70, 472, 484.

130. Cf. Radzinowicz, *History of English Criminal Law*, pp. 25–88.

131. *Ibid.*, pp. 151–52.

132. *Ibid.*, p. 159.

133. *Ibid.*, p. 497 ff.

134. On predecessors of Romilly, in particular the Parliamentary Committee of 1750 and its recommendations, see Radzinowicz, *ibid.*, pp. 415–21.

135. Howard, *State of Prisons in England and Wales*.

136. There was one execution for treason during the First World War. During the Second World War, there were two executions for treason and fifteen under the Treachery Act, 1940 (Royal Commission, *Report*, Sec. 18, p. 5).

137. *Ibid.*, pp. 300–1, table 1.

138. By the Murder (Abolition of Death Penalty) Act 1965.

139. This is a nearly total abolition. However, it does not extend to treason, piracy with violence, arsons at dockyards, and certain naval and military crimes.

5. WHY DOES THE LAW BECOME LESS HARSH

1. On its emergence, see chapter 4, note 12, *supra*.

2. On the wealth of these experiential data, see my *Theory of Criminal Justice*, pp. 138–39, notes 20–21.

3. For an analysis of how these two mechanisms interact, see *ibid.*, pp. 11–12.

4. By the "most advanced form" I mean awareness understood as verbal comprehension of correct contingencies of punishment (or reinforcement). Some kind of nonverbal "comprehension" may be present among animals and especially among primates, as claimed by Gestalt psychologists (cf., in particular, Kohler, *Mentality of Apes*. For an excellent summary of critical appraisals of Kohler's and related views, see Berlyne, *Structure and Direction in Thinking*, pp. 329–46). The rather vague issue of evolutionary emergence and advancement of symbolic capacities may be clarified and answered in a publicly convincing way by future progress in the biochemistry of our nervous system. As one optimistic theorist of thinking claims, "there must be psychological, physiological, and ultimately physicochemical laws whose action is manifest throughout the spectrum of behavior from the crudest to the loftiest. *We shall, no doubt, eventually understand* how a nervous system evolving in certain directions must sooner or later reach a level at which symbolic capacities come into existence, and how symbolic capacities, having advanced to a particular stage, must give rise to thinking (Berlyne, *ibid.*, p. 6, emphasis added).

5. Parke, "Role of Punishment," pp. 86–87.

6. That is, punishment following an act that is itself instrumental in bringing reward, e.g., spanking a child after he has eaten prohibited candy.

7. Cf., e.g., Glueck and Glueck, *Unraveling Juvenile Delinquency*, p. 131; McCord, McCord, and Zola, *Origins of Crime*, pp. 76–79, 101–3, 154–55.

8. Cf. Sears, Maccoby, and Levin, *Patterns of Child Rearing*, pp. 172–73.

9. For instance, by Brown and Wagner, "Resistance to Punishment and Extinction," p. 503; Banks, "Persistence to Continuous Punishment," p. 373; Banks, "Persistence to Continuous Punishment and Nonreward," p. 105; Deur and Parke, "Resistance to Extinction and Continuous Punishment," p. 91. Cf. also the well-known study by A. E. Fisher, referred to by Parke, "Role of Punishment," p. 99.

10. Amsel, "Role of Frustrative Nonreward," p. 102; "Frustrative Nonreward," p. 306; "Partial Reinforcement Effects," pp. 1–65; Wagner, "Frustration and Punishment," pp. 229–39; Banks, "Persistence to Continuous Punishment," p. 373; Parke, Deur, and Sawin, "Intermittent Punishment Effect," p. 193; Linden, "Transfer of Approach Responding," p. 498.

11. "[O]ne boundary condition . . . is that the punishment has to be introduced in such a way that the goal response is not completely inhibited during acquisition" (Martin, "Reward and Punishment," p. 441).

12. Cf. Petrażycki, *Wstep do nauki polityki prawa*, pp. 330–34.

13. Cf. chapter 4, text to notes 15, 52–54, and 70, *supra*.

14. Cf., e.g., Hippel, *Deutsches Strafrecht*, 1:145; 2:289.

15. Petrażycki, *Wstep do nauki polityki prawa*, p. 329.

16. Cf. chapter 4, text to notes 31, 32, and 51, *supra*.

17. If, on the other hand, the ideas are of a past and, moreover, wrong conduct, the experience of the previously broken duty is known as "guilt"— a familiar feeling of one's bad conscience or of someone else's being guilty of wrongdoing.

18. Cf. my *Theory of Criminal Justice*, pp. 4–5. The notions of counter-action and provocation, as well as distinctions made in the preceding paragraph, come from a modified version of Petrażycki's theory. (The modification consists, in particular, in the rejection of his unusual demarcation line between law and morality.) Cf. Petrażycki, *Law and Morality*, pp. 14, 31–62, and my "Leon Petrażycki," pp. 5–6.

19. Cf. my *Theory of Criminal Justice*, pp. 6, 18.

20. This perception of criminal law as an implement of the society's moral education requires a note of caution. It would be easy to overstate the point and to assume that the law may become a primary force that shapes moral views of society. Consequently, one might claim that by introducing new criminal prohibitions,we can arbitrarily change the dominant moral sentiment or that by simply keeping the old ones in force we can prevent the sentiment from changing. Indeed, assumptions of this kind have had some influence in various societies. For instance, in England and in this country, keeping some clearly victimless crimes on the law books has been recommended in order to "preserve [the existing] moral code" (Devlin, *Enforcement of Morals*, p. 13; cf. also "Reservation by Mr. Adair," in *The Wolfenden Report*, p. 197/VI), that is, to prevent the supposedly ominous moral change—in this case, the spread of the radically utilitarian claim that acts that do not cause anyone to suffer are not wrong.

These assumptions are unfounded. As the preceding analysis should make clear, the sources of any society's moral sentiment are many and complex, and learning by criminal sanctions constitutes but one of them. Moreover, the sanctions are always a "secondary" source; to be morally effective, a sanction must be imposed for behavior already widely experienced as morally wrong.

21. Cf. Radzinowicz, *History of English Criminal Law*, pp. 425–26, 588–89.

22. Quoted after Radzinowicz, *ibid.*, p. 292. The general idea of law as an implement of moral learning should not be limited to the norms of criminal law. Other parts of the legal system, such as law of contracts, torts, or family law, may also play a similar educative role, and, as powerfully stressed by Petrażycki, they have played it through the history of various societies. Thus, the law of Athens and, much more so, the Roman law and the modern legal systems have sanctioned indecency in entering and performing contracts. The sanctions consisted, for instance, in invalidity of contracts entered under du-

ress or deceit and of usurious or otherwise turpitudinous contracts, and in damages for nonperformance, as well as liability for concealed defects of the property sold. The law of property has rewarded the *bonae fidei* possessor with direct acquisition of ownership from nonowner or acquisition through usucapion and with advantages in appropriating fruits of someone else's real property. The Roman law of delicts, as well as the common law of torts, sanctioned, by damages, a long list of private wrongs, whereas many laws of continental Europe, following the ingeniousness of the French doctrine, adopted a general norm—whoever causes, through his fault, damage to another person is duty bound to repair it (cf., in particular, Art. 1382 of the *Code Napoléon*). The law of succession has punished, by exclusion from inheritance, various wrongs against the deceased. (A unique comparative analysis of various forms of the exclusion from inheritance has been provided by Gwiazdomorski, *Law of Inheritance*, pp. 67–73, 382–404.)

With respect to all kinds of legal claims, the ancient principles—"nemo turpitudinem suam allegans, audiatur" and "he who comes into equity must come with clean hands"—punished depravity by denial of access and rewarded innocence by granting access to courts. A specific application of these principles emerged, as the rule of recrimination, in various family laws: the rule prevents those guilty of disrupting their marriages from effectively claiming divorce. (See on this my "Moral Premises of Contemporary Divorce Laws," pp. 124–30; "Recrimination in Eastern Europe," p. 617.) As these instances imply, not only criminal law but also legal norms of all kinds have been most significant here; their function consists exactly in explicit sanctioning of wrongdoing.

23. See chapter 1, note 5, *supra*.

24. The disgust would be predominantly but not exclusively moral; it would constitute an aesthetic aversion as well. Apparently to arouse both moral and aesthetic aversion, some abolitionists suggested, in the 1960s, that executions be televised; they hoped that in effect the public support for the death penalty "would soon dwindle" (90th Congress, 2nd Session, U.S. Senate, *To Abolish the Death Penalty*, p. 40).

25. Bandura, "Analysis of Modeling Processes," p. 51.

26. Montesquieu, *Spirit of Laws*, 1:123.

27. Beccaria, *On Crimes and Punishments*, p. 43.

28. Radzinowicz, *History of English Criminal Law*, p. 38.

29. Petrażycki, *Wstęp do nauki polityki prawa*, p. 40.

30. The fallacy consists in the belief of some functional theorists that all accepted forms of culture, and especially all accepted ideas, moral or otherwise, work as adaptive tools: they fulfill essential needs of society. On the obvious shortcomings of this belief, see, e.g., Merton, *Social Theory*, pp. 84–86; Hempel, *Aspects of Scientific Explanation*, 1965, p. 322; Ossowska, *Social Determinants*, p. 104.

31. Cf. chapter 4, text to notes 112–14 and 118–21, *supra*.

32. Montesquieu, *Spirit of Laws*, 1:118.

33. Cf. chapter 4, note 5, *supra*.

6. ABOLITIONIST TREND

1. Cf. Friedman, *History of American Law*, p. 611.
2. Cf. Spear, *Punishment of Death*, pp. 227–31.
3. Horowitz, *Capital Punishment, U.S.A.*, p. 41.
4. Friedman, *History of American Law*, p. 76.
5. Cf. chapter 4, text to notes 121–22, *supra*.
6. Cf. chapter 1, note 19, *supra*.
7. Meltsner, *Cruel and Unusual*, p. 47.
8. For a more detailed review of the developments outlined in this paragraph, see Filler, "Movements to Abolish Death Penalty," pp. 124–36; and Davis, "Movement to Abolish Capital Punishment," pp. 23–46. For samples of views of all leading abolitionists in the United States, from Benjamin Rush to Hugo Adam Bedau, cf. Mackey, *Voices Against Death*.
9. U.S. Senate, *To Abolish the Death Penalth*, p. 14. Whether the quotation comes from Jefferson is uncertain. According to a personal communication from Professor Bedau, Julian Boyd was sure the quotation was apocryphal. Cf. also Bedau, "Death Penalty in America," p. 36; and Mackey, *Voices Against Death*, pp. 97–98, who attributes the quotation to Lafayette.
10. Cf. Mackey, *ibid.*, pp. 17–18.
11. Meltsner, *Cruel and Unusual*, p. 48.
12. *Ibid.*
13. Davis, "Movement to Abolish Capital Punishment," p. 33.
14. On the influence of this idea on the law of Pennsylvania, see Barnes, *Story of Punishment*, pp. 105–6, 109.
15. See Davis, "Movement to Abolish Capital Punishment," p. 35.
16. *Ibid.*, p. 30.
17. *Ibid.*, p. 31; Mackey, *Voices Against Death*, pp. 71–76.
18. See this chapter, note 50, *infra*.
19. Friedman, *History of American Law*, p. 250.
20. Filler, "Movements to Abolish Death Penalty," p. 124.
21. Cf. Bowers, *Executions in America*, p. 8, table 1–2.
22. Cf., e.g., Meltsner, *Cruel and Unusual*, p. 48; Bedau, *Death Penalty in America* (Anchor Books), pp. 28–29; Mackey, "Inutility of Mandatory Capital Punishment," pp. 32–35. On other kinds of discretionary evasion of mandatory death sentences, cf. Bedau, "Felony-Murder Rape," pp. 493–520.
23. Meltsner, *Cruel and Unusual*, p. 51.
24. Friedman, *History of American Law*, pp. 252, 518.
25. Cf. Bowers, *Executions in America* pp. 5, 29.
26. For their long list and a skilled analysis of their activities, see Meltsner, *Cruel and Unusual*, *passim*.
27. Cf., e.g., statements by Donald E. J. MacNamara, Jerome Frank, and Edwin Barchard, in Bedau, *Death Penalty in America* (Anchor Books), p. 189; Sara R. Ehrmann, *ibid.*, pp. 501–14; Radzinowicz in U.S. Senate, *To Abolish the Death Penalty*, pp. 59–60; James V. Bennett, *ibid.*, pp. 33–34; G. Mennen William, *ibid.*, p. 52.
28. Cf. Bedau, *Death Penalty in America* (Anchor Books), p. 407; Sara R. Ehrmann, in *ibid.*, pp. 505–13.

29. This holds true of earlier inquiries undertaken to corroborate the claim (especially Sellin's "Homicides," pp. 135–54) and of those more recent aiming at its refutation, most notably by Ehrlich ("Deterrent Effect of Capital Punishment," p. 397.) For rejoinder, see, in particular, Passell, "Deterrent Effect of Death Penalty," p. 61; Bowers and Pierce, "Illusion of Deterrence," p. 187; Passell and Taylor, "Deterrent Effect of Capital Punishment," p. 445; Klein, Frost, and Filatov, "Deterrent Effect of Capital Punishment," in Bedau, *Death Penalty in America* [Oxford], pp. 138–59.

30. Cf., in particular, the views of the clergymen subcommittee of the Massachusetts Investigating Committee of 1960, Bedau, *Death Penalty in America*, p. 516; Radzinowicz in U.S. Senate, *To Abolish the Death Penalty*, p. 66; New York Committee to Abolish Capital Punishment, *ibid.*, p. 166.

31. For a sample of the descriptions, Bedau, *Courts, Constitution, and Capital Punishment*, pp. 101–2.

32. Clinton Duffy, former warden of San Quentin, in U.S. Senate, *To Abolish the Death Penalty*, p. 21.

33. Louis J. West, in *ibid.*, p. 125.

34. In the mid-1960s, the average period spent on the death row amounted to 32.6 months, but in several record cases it exceeded 13 years (Bedau, *Courts, Constitution, and Capital Punishment*, pp. 60, 139).

35. Sacco and Vanzetti's and Caryl Chessman's being among the most famous of these cases.

36. Donald E. J. MacNamara's words, referred to by Bedau, *Death Penalty in America*, p. 187.

37. Herbert B. Ehrmann, in *ibid.*, p. 433; cf. President's Commission, *Challenge of Crime*, p. 143.

38. Cf. chapter 7, text to notes 1–4, *infra*; see also my *Theory of Criminal Justice*, pp. 68–71.

39. Bedau, *Death Penalty in America* 1967, p. 240.

40. See my *Theory of Criminal Justice*, pp. 74–75.

41. Donald E. J. MacNamara, in Bedau, *Death Penalty in America*, p. 183.

42. Joyce Vialet, quoting former Governor DiSalle, in U.S. Senate, *To Abolish the Death Penalty*, p. 182. For similar views of many others, see *ibid.*, pp. 11, 96, 98–99, 123, 125; see also President's Commission, *Challenge of Crime*, p. 143.

43. Cf., e.g., U.S. Senate, *To Abolish the Death Penalty*, pp. 93, 96, 98–99, 108, 123.

44. Cf. Wolfgang and Riedel, "Race, Racial Discrimination and Death Penalty," pp. 119–33; Bowers, *Executions in America*, pp. 109–20.

45. Cf. U.S. Senate, *To Abolish the Death Penalty*, pp. 84, 88, 166.

46. *Criminal Justice Statistics 1974*, 1975, p. 223, table 2–109.

47. *Criminal Justice Statistics 1978*, 1979, p. 326, table 2–65.

48. Harris Poll, referred to by Erskine, "Polls: Capital Punishment," p. 295.

49. Strictly speaking, as the following note implies, of five states and one territory—the Virgin Islands.

50. The six legislatures abolished the death penalty in Alaska, Hawaii, Virgin Islands, West Virginia, Oregon, and Iowa. (Delaware also abolished the death penalty in 1958, only to restore it three years later.) The two nearly abolitionist

states were Vermont and New York. The supreme courts implemented abolition in New Jersey and California. The historical development of the whole list was as follows:

Abolition of Death Penalties in the United States, 1846–1972

Jurisdiction	Date of Abolition	Date of Restoration	Date of Reabolition
Michigan	1846[a]		
Rhode Island	1852[b]		
Wisconsin	1853		
Iowa	1872	1878	1965
Maine	1876[c]	1883	1887
Colorado	1897	1901	
Kansas	1907[d]	1935	
Minnesota	1911		
Washington	1913	1919	
Oregon	1914	1920	1964
North Dakota	1915[e]		
South Dakota	1915	1939	
Tennessee	1915[f]	1919	
Arizona	1916	1918	
Missouri	1917	1919	
Puerto Rico	1917	1919	1929
Alaska	1957		
Hawaii	1957		
Virgin Islands	1957		
Delaware	1958	1961	
West Virginia	1965		
Vermont	1965[g]		
New York	1965[h]		
New Jersey	1972[i]		
California	1972[i]		

Source: National Prisoner Statistics 1930–1970, 1971, table 16 (except for abolition in New Jersey and California).

Explanations:

[a] Death penalty retained for treason until 1963.
[b] Death penalty restored in 1882 for any life term convict who commits murder.
[c] In 1837 a law was passed to provide that no condemned person could be executed until one year after his sentencing and then only upon a warrant from the governor.
[d] In 1872 a law was passed similar to the 1837 Maine statute (see note c above)
[e] Death penalty retained for muder by a prisoner serving a life term for murder.
[f] Death penalty retained for rape.
[g] Death penalty retained for murder of a policeman or guard or by a prisoner guilty of a prior murder.
[h] Death penalty retained for murder of a police officer on duty, or of anyone by a prisoner under life sentence.
[i] Death penalty abolished by state supreme court decision.

51. See Bowers, *Executions in America*, p. 8, table 1–2; on the few exceptions, see Bedau, *Death Penalty in America* 1967, pp. 47–52.

52. Executions in the United States 1947–68 (Source: *National Prisoner Statistics—Capital Punishment 1930–1968*, No. 45, August 1969, table 1):

Year	1947	1948	1949	1950	1951	1952	1953	1954	1955	1956	1957
Total executions	153	119	119	82	105	83	62	81	76	65	65

Year	1958	1959	1960	1961	1962	1963	1964	1965	1966	1967	1968
Total executions	49	49	56	42	47	21	15	7	1	2	0

53. For instance, several of the most brutal murders in New Jersey resulted in the court's accepting either a plea of *nolo contendere* because a jury simply could not be impaneled or in a life sentence despite the prosecutor's urging in the strongest language for the death penalty (Bedau, *Death Penalty in America*, p. 409); see, e.g., State v. Wolak (Passaic County, 1959), State v. Driver (Mercer County, 1961), State v. Siegel (Monmouth County, 1961), and State v. Maxey and Parks (Union County, 1961).

54. Bowers, *Executions in America*, p. 12.

55. Admissions to death row in the United States, 1960–68 (Source: *National Prisoner Statistics—Executions 1930–1966*, No. 41, April 1967, and *Executions 1930–1967*, No. 42, June 1968):

Year	1960	1961	1962	1963	1964	1965	1966	1967	1968
Total admissions	113	140	103	93	106	86	118	85	102

56. Bowers, *Executions in America*, p. 12.

57. See note 55, *supra*.

58. See note 52, *supra*.

59. Michael Meltsner, by publishing his *Cruel and Unusual*, became not only an active participant in this struggle but also its best historian.

60. *Ibid.*, pp. 90–93.

61. *Ibid.*, p. 107.

62. *National Prisoner Statistics—Capital Punishment 1930–1968*, No. 45, August 1969, table 4.

63. Bowers, *Executions in America*, pp. 12, 28.

64. See note 52, *supra*.

65. *National Prisoner Statistics—Capital Punishment 1930–1966*, No. 41, April 1967, figure F.

66. *National Prisoner Statistics—Capital Punishment 1977*, November 1978, table 6.

67. Thorsten Sellin in U.S. Senate, *To Abolish the Death Penalty*, p. 81.

68. Heline, *Capital Punishment*, p. 7.

69. Horowitz, *Capital Punishment, U.S.A.*, p. 8.

70. Cf. the hearings before the Subcommittee on Criminal Laws and Procedures of the U.S. Senate (*To Abolish the Death Penalty*) as a visible display of the pressure on and within the Congress.

71. Weems v. United States, 217 U.S. 349 (1910).

72. Cf. Rubin, *Law of Criminal Correction*, pp. 438–41; the quotation comes from pp. 440–41. See, however, In re Lynch, 8 Cal. 3d 410 (1972).

73. Trop v. Dulles, 356 U.S. 86, 100 (1958).

74. 370 U.S. 660 (1962).

75. Cf., e.g., Jordan v. Fitzharris, 257 F. Supp. 674 (N.D. Cal. 1966); Lollis v. New York State Dept. of Social Servies, 327 F. Supp. 473 (S.D.N.Y. 1970). For an instance of the Eighth Amendment challenge of appalling conditions of a solitary confinement rather than of the confinement itself, see Wright v. McMann, 387 F. 2d 519 (2d Cir. 1967).

76. Cf., in particular, Jackson v. Bishop, 404 F. 2d 571 (8th Cir. 1968); Gonzalez v. Rockefeller, *Criminal Law Reporter* 10:2227 (2d Cir., Dec. 1, 1971).

77. Knecht v. Gillman, 488 F. 2d 1136 (8th Cir. 1973).

78. Cf., e.g., Pisciano v. State, 8 App. Div. 2d 335, 340, 188 N.Y.S. 2d 35, 40 (1959); Newman v. State, 349 F. Supp. 278 (M. D. Ala. 1972).

79. For a landmark case, see Holt v. Sarver, 309 F. Supp. 362 (E. D. Ark. 1970), *aff'd* 442 F. 2d 304 (8th Cir. 1971).

80. Wilkerson v. Utah, 99 U.S. 130 (1878).

81. State v. Gee Jon, 46 Nev. 418, 211 P. 676, 217 P. 587, 30 A.L.R. 1443 (1923).

82. In re Kemmler, 136 U.S. 436 (1889).

83. Louisiana ex rel. Francis v. Resweber, 329 U.S. 459 (1947).

84. See, in particular, Gerald H. Gottlieb, "Testing the Death Penalty," pp. 264, 281; Rubin, "Supreme Court," pp. 121–31; Goldberg and Dershowitz, "Declaring Death Penalty Unconstitutional," pp. 1773–1819.

85. In Rudolph v. Alabama, 375 U.S. 889 (1963). Justices Brennan and Douglas joined in the dissent.

86. In Boykin v. Alabama, 395 U.S. 238 (1969).

7. WHY THE REVERSAL?

1. Chapter 6, text to note 38, *supra*.

2. President's Commission, p. 15.

3. Words of Clarence Darrow, after Mitford, *Kind and Usual Punishment*, p. 297.

4. Clark, *Crime in America*, p. 67.

5. Gorecki, "Crime Causation Theories," p. 464.

6. Wilson, *Thinking about Crime*, p. 52.

7. See my *Theory of Criminal Justice*, pp. 74–81.

8. Martinson, "What Works?" pp. 22, 25.

9. In various primitive societies, the perceived certainty is not necessarily a function of how certain the punishments indeed are—primitive religious beliefs and superstition may produce a highly inflated perception (cf. chapter 5, text to note 15, *supra*). Misperceptions also easily occur in closed societies where authoritarian governments arrest communications. On the other hand, in modern societies enjoying free flow of information, there is no way of hiding how certain or how intermittent punishment of criminals is, and whatever confusion on this issue may temporarily occur, it always tends to disappear.

10. Cf. chapter 5, text following note 19, *supra*.

11. Cf. chapter 5, text to note 20, *supra*.

12. For a more detailed analysis of these forces, see my *Theory of Criminal Justice*, pp. 63–89.

13. FBI, *Uniform Crime Reports 1976*, 1977, p. 162, table 20, and p. 217, table 54; *Uniform Crime Reports 1980*, 1981, p. 182, table 20.

14. The FBI-reported crimes include murder, forcible rape, robbery, aggravated assault, larceny-theft, and motor-vehicle theft.

15. This is a conclusion from victimization survey statistics; cf. *Sourcebook of Criminal Justice Statistics 1980*, 1981, p. 228, table 3.1.

16. Cf. Hood and Sparks, "Citizens' Attitudes and Police Practice," p. 173.

17. Zimring and Hawkins, *Deterrence*, p. 336.

18. On injustices other than those caused by arbitrariness, see my *Theory of Criminal Justice*, pp. 31–43.

19. See *ibid.*, pp. 32–33.

20. In Santobello v. New York, 404 U.S. 257 (1971); cf. Brady v. United States, 397 U.S. 742 (1970).

21. See, e.g., estimates by Newman, *Conviction*, p. 3; and by the President's Commission, *Task Force Report*, p. 9.

22. Moley, "Vanishing Jury," pp. 97, 119.

23. For a more detailed analysis of these and other effects of plea bargaining, see my *Theory of Criminal Justice*, pp. 50–62.

24. I owe the qualification of the last two sentences to the criticism by Wertheimer, Book Review, pp. 1169–71.

25. Cf., e.g., Alschuler, "Defense Attorney's Role," pp. 1179, 1247–48.

26. That is why the Supreme Court stresses the weight of defense counsel's presence at plea negotiations, and legislative changes have been recommended to make the negotiations equally available to all defendants and scrutinized by judges (see President's Commission, *Task Force Report*, pp. 12–13; American Bar Association, *Standards Relating to Pleas of Guilty*, pp. 10–12; cf. also American Law Institute, *Model Code*, p. 62). Some of the recommendations have been embodied in the 1974 Amendment of the Federal Rule of Criminal Procedure 11.

27. Cf. Alschuler, "Defense Attorney's Role," pp. 1231–36.

28. President's Commission, *Task Force Report*, p. 11

29. Blumberg, *Criminal Justice*, p. 89.

30. This does not imply that there would be anything wrong in imposing

on a suspect or witness questioned about a dangerous kind of crime a legal duty to provide information that he has and in energetically enforcing this duty by criminal penalties in the event of his refusal or misinformation.

31. Rosett and Cressey, *Justice by Consent*, p. 43.

32. *Sourcebook 1980*, 1981, p. 290, table 3.51, p. 291, figure 3.23.

33. FBI, *Uniform Crime Reports 1980*, 1981, pp. 7, 14, 16, 20.

34. See note 15, *supra*.

35. FBI, *Uniform Crime Reports 1980*, 1981, pp. 17, 24, 28.

36. *Sourcebook 1980*, 1981, p. 4, table 1.3.

37. "The Losing Battle Against Crime in America," *U.S. News and World Report*, Dec. 16, 1974, p. 32.

38. New York *Times*, July 7, p. 7 (and July 3, p. 7); San Francisco Chronicle, July 3, p. 1, July 4, p. 14, July 6, p. 8.

39. New York *Times*, July 4, p. 9.

40. *Ibid.*, July 7, pp. 1. 10, July 8, p. 11; Chicago Tribune, July 7, p. 3.

41. Chicago *Tribune*, July 5, p. 12.

42. New York *Times*, July 2, p. 12, July 6, p. 11; Chicago *Tribune*, July 1, p.5.

43. James Q. Wilson, *Thinking About Crime*, p. 21.

44. For instances, see Stinchcombe and Associates, *Crime and Punishment*, p. X. Cf. also Thomas and Foster, "Public Support for Capital Punishment," pp. 641, 646–55.

45. For skillful use of both kinds of data to test the guess, see Stinchcombe and Associates, *Crime and Punishment*, pp. 39–73.

46. Cf., e.g., *Sourcebook 1980*, 1981, p. 172, table 2.6.

47. *Sourcebook of Criminal Justice Statistics 1979*, 1980, pp. 260–61, tables 2.10, 2.11, 2.12.

48. *Sourcebook 1980*, 1981, p. 174, table 2.7.

49. *Sourcebook of Criminal Justice Statistics 1974*, 1975, pp. 204–5, table 2.71, and *Sourcebook 1980*, 1981, pp. 196–97, table 2.32.

50. *Sourcebook 1974*, 1975, p. 223, table 2.109, and *Sourcebook 1980*, 1981, pp. 200–1, table 2.33.

51. This causal relationship may feasibly work through any of the following processes: first, an increasing proportion of the total population is afraid and, therefore, punitive; second, those afraid experience stronger fear and, therefore, an increasing proportion of them becomes punitive; or, third, both processes, the first and the second, occur simultaneously.

52. Stinchcombe and Associates, *Crime and Punishment*, pp. 68–69.

53. *Ibid.*, pp. 11, 68–69, 100.

54. *Sourcebook 1980*, 1981, pp. 200–1, table 2.33.

55. *Sourcebook of Criminal Justice Statistics 1978*, 1979, p. 329, table 2.72. Cf. also, for a 1974 survey, Ellsworth and Ross, "Public Opinion and Judicial Decision Making," p. 168.

56. 0.35:0.60 = 0.38; 0.46:0.67 = 0.68.

57. See text to note 48, *supra*.

58. Having questioned, in the winter of 1973–74, a Norfolk, Virginia, sample of heads of households, Charles W. Thomas concluded that there are two main reasons for public support for the death penalty, the strongest reason being the wish to deter, and the second strongest being the demand for retribution (Thomas, "Eighth Amendment Challenges," pp. 1005, 1016–30; Thomas and Howard, "Public Attitudes Toward Capital Punishment," pp. 189, 197–209). This conclusion, even if valid, does not contradict my stand (and the validity of the conclusion may be debated because of the study's limited geographical scope and the low rate of return of completed questionnaires). First, Thomas compared the relative impact of the wish to deter vs. demand for retribution, as opposed to comparing the impact of fear vs. anger. The difference between the two comparisons is essential. In particular, advocacy of capital punishment caused by belief in its power to deter does not necessarily imply fear—those unafraid may also wish to apply the death penalty to deter wrongdoers. Furthermore, Thomas' inquiry asks about determinants for punitive attitudes on the day of the inquiry, whereas this chapter asks about determinants for the change of punitive attitudes throughout several years.

59. This explanation disregards the impact of individual attitudes on punitiveness. The impact has been claimed by various personality psychologists. They maintain that punitiveness and, in particular, favoring the death penalty are associated with authoritarianism, extreme conservatism, lack of education, rigidity, dogmatism, intolerance, prejudice, etc. (For a critical review of these claims, see Vidmar and Ellsworth, "Public Opinion and Death Penalty," pp. 1245, 1258–62; Thomas and Foster, "Public Support for Capital Punishment," pp. 642–44, 654.)

This psychological account is irrelevant for my explanation of the spread of punitive attitudes in America. Moreover, irrespective of whether the account is valid or not (and its validity has been challenged), its use by the abolitionists arouses doubts. First, it sounds preposterous to say to anyone on the ground of rather vague assumptions: I know better than you why you think as you do. Second, there is a certain, apparently unintentional, unfairness to the account: to imply that retentionists are unwise, backward, and personally defective may simply scare some of them from expressing their views, and this is not how the struggle for abolition should proceed.

60. *Sourcebook 1978*, 1979, p. 326, table 2.65.

61. *Ibid.*, p. 329, table 2.69. (For rape and mugging, the proportion changed insignificantly; for skyjacking—a crime brought under control between 1973 and 1977—the proportion declined from 27 percent to 22 percent.)

62. For a striking (and rather extreme) instance, see Berns, *For Capital Punishment*. Berns directs his anger, first, at criminals: capital punishment should sanction the most heinous crimes and executions should be public. He also directs his anger at opponents of capital punishment; in his view, they advocate "a world without dignity, without morality, and indifferent of how we live" (p. 163). For a few other important instances, cf. Bedau, "Death Penalty in the United States," pp. 63–64.

63. The society's changing views reach the Court largely indirectly—they are transmitted, in particular, through the other branches of government, especially congressional committees and state legislatures, through accounts coming from state judges and chief justices, through the word expressed by a variety of nongovernmental groups advocating legal policies and ideas, and by individuals from the bar, the law schools, the press, and the general political establishment. The thus transmitted views are often critical of the Court's decisions; "from John Marshall's day onward a tide of critical commentary has run—of varying degrees of respectfulness" (Paul A. Freund, *Supreme Court*, p. 171).

64. The expression is Petrażycki's.

65. See data referred to in note 49, *supra*.

66. See data referred to in note 50, *supra*.

67. *Ibid.*

68. See data referred to in note 49, *supra*.

69. See data referred to in note 50, *supra*.

70. Cf. text to note 61, *supra*.

71. Cf. text to note 55, *supra*.

8. FUTURE DEVELOPMENTS

1. Cf. chapter 5, text to note 31, *supra*.

2. Cf. chapter 3, text to notes 11 and 12, *supra*.

3. Lummus, *Trial Judge*, p. 46.

4. Cf. Breitel, "Controls in Criminal Law Enforcement," pp. 427, 428.

5. This ninety-years'-long habituation is the main reason why Heumann (in *Plea Bargaining*, pp. 157–62) concludes, on the ground of an empirical inquiry conducted in Connecticut, that the abolition of plea bargaining is impossible. For similar reasons, in a personal communication, Professor Edward Sagarin calls the view that plea bargaining can be abolished, utopian—"a wonderful world . . . completely out of reach, at least in the forseeable America." One important reason why the removal of plea bargaining may be, indeed, utopian today is that it is widely perceived as utopian. It is hoped that these and the following comments will help to undermine this perception.

6. In *Theory of Criminal Justice*, pp. 93–132.

7. See *ibid.*

8. I owe this perception of the Stoic ideas to the late Jerzy Lande's lectures on Philosophy of Law held (at the Jagiellonian University in Cracow) in 1946–47. Cf. also his *Studies in Philosophy of Law*, pp. 484–87.

BIBLIOGRAPHY

Alschuler, Albert W. "The Defense Attorney's Role in Plea Bargaining." *Yale L. J.* (1975) 84:1179.

American Bar Association Project on Minimum Standards for Criminal Justice. *Standards Relating to Pleas of Guilty*. Approved Draft, 1968.

American Law Institute. *A Model Code of Pre-Arraignment Procedure*. Tentative Draft No. 5, 1972.

Amsel, A. "The Role of Frustrative Nonreward in Noncontinuous Reward Situations." *Psychological Bulletin* (1958) 55:102.

—— "Frustrative Nonreward in Partial Reinforcement and Discrimination Learning: Some Recent History and a Theoretical Extension." *Psychological Review* (1962) 69:306.

—— "Partial Reinforcement Effects on Vigor and Persistence." In K. W. Spence and J. T. Spence, eds., *The Psychology of Learning and Motivation: Advances in Research and Theory*, vol. 1. New York: Academic Press, 1967, pp. 1–65.

Ancel, Marc. *La défense sociale nouvelle*. Paris: Éditions Cujas, 1966.

Arkin, Steven D. "Discrimination and Arbitrariness in Capital Punishment: An Analysis of Post-*Furman* Murder Cases in Dade County, Florida, 1973–1976." *Stanford L. R.* (1980) 33:75.

Baldus, David C., Charles A. Pulaski, Jr., George Woodworth, and Frederick D. Kyle. "Identifying Comparatively Excessive Sentences of Death: A Quantitative Approach." *Stanford L. R.* (1980) 33:1.

Bandura, Albert. "Analysis of Modeling Processes." In Albert Bandura, ed., *Psychological Modeling*. Chicago: Aldine, 1971.

Banks, R. K. "Persistence to Continuous Punishment Following Intermittent Punishment Training." *J. Of Experimental Psychology* (1966) 71:373.

—— "Persistence to Continuous Punishment and Nonreward Following Training with Intermittent Punishment and Nonreward." *Psychonomic Science* (1966) 5:105.

Barkan, Irving. *Capital Punishment in Ancient Athens.* Chicago, 1936.

Barnes, Harry Elmer. *The Story of Punishment.* Montclair, N.J.: Patterson Smith, 1972.

Beccaria, Cesare. *On Crimes and Punishments.* Indianapolis: Bobbs-Merrill, 1963.

Bedau, Hugo Adam. *The Courts, the Constitution, and Capital Punishment.* Lexington, Mass.: Lexington Books, 1977.

—— *The Death Penalty in America.* Garden City, N.Y.: Anchor Books, 1967.

—— *The Death Penalty in America.* Oxford: Oxford University Press, 1982.

—— "The Death Penalty in America." *Federal Probation* (June 1971) 35:32.

—— "The Death Penalty in the United States: Imposed Law and the Role of Moral Elites." In S. B. Burman and B. E. Harrell-Bond, eds., *The Imposition of Law.* New York: Academic Press, 1979, pp. 45–68.

—— "Felony-Murder Rape and the Mandatory Death Penalty: A Study in Discretionary Justice." *Suffolk Univ. L. R.* (1976) 10:493.

Berlyne, D. E. *Structure and Direction in Thinking.* New York: John Wiley, 1965.

Berns, Walter. *For Capital Punishment.* New York: Basic Books, 1979.

Black, Charles L., Jr. *Capital Punishment: The Inevitability of Caprice and Mistake.* New York: W. W. Norton, 1974.

—— "The Death Penalty Now." *Tulane L. R.* (1977) 51:429.

—— "Due Process for Death: *Jurek v. Texas* and Companion Cases." *Catholic University L. R.* (1977) 26:1.

Blackstone's *Commentaries on the Laws of England,* vol. IV.

Blumberg, Abraham S. *Criminal Justice.* New York: New Viewpoints, 1974.

Bonner, Robert J. and Gertrude Smith. *The Administration of Justice from Homer to Aristotle.* New York: AMS Press, 1970.

Bouzat, Pierre and Jean Pinatel. *Traité de droit pénal et de criminologie.* Paris: Librarie Dalloz, 1970.

Bowers, William J. *Executions in America.* Lexington, Mass.: Lexington Books, 1974.

Bowers, William J. and Glenn L. Pierce. "Arbitrariness and Discrimination Under Post-*Furman* Capital Statutes." *Crime and Delinquency* (1980) 26:563.

—— "The Illusion of Deterrence in Isaac Ehrlich's Research on Capital Punishment." *Yale L. J.* (1975) 85:187.

Breitel, Charles D. "Controls in Criminal Law Enforcement." *Chicago L. R.* (1960) 27:427.

Brown, R. T. and A. R. Wagner. "Resistance to Punishment and Extinction Following Training with Shock or Nonreinforcement." *J. of Experimental Psychology* (1964) 68:503.

Browning, James R. "The New Death Penalty Statutes: Perpetuating a Costly Myth." *Gonzaga L. R.* (1974) 9:651.

Chambliss, William J. "A Sociological Analysis of the Law of Vagrancy." *Social Problems* (1964) 12:67.

Clark, Ramsey. *Crime in America*. New York: Simon and Schuster, 1970.

Davis, David Brion. "The Movement to Abolish Capital Punishment in America, 1787–1861." *American Historical Review* (October 1957) 63:23.

Deur, Jan L. and Ross D. Parke. "Resistance to Extinction and Continuous Punishment in Humans as a Function of Partial Reward and Partial Punishment Training." *Psychonomic Science* (1968) 13:91.

Devlin, Patrick. *The Enforcement of Morals*. London: Oxford University Press, 1965.

Diamond, A. S. *Primitive Law Past and Present*. London: Methuen, 1971.

Dix, George E. "Administration of the Texas Death Penalty Statutes: Constitutional Infirmities Related to the Prediction of Dangerousness." *Texas L.R.* (1977) 55:1343.

—— "Appellate Review of the Decision to Impose Death." *Georgetown L. J.* (1979) 68:97.

Donnelly, Samuel J. M. "A Theory of Justice, Judicial Methodology, and the Constitutionality of Capital Punishment: Rawls, Dworkin, and a Theory of Criminal Responsibility." *Syracuse L. R.* (1978) 29:1109.

Durkheim, Emile. "Two Laws of Penal Evolution." In Mark Traugott, ed., *Emile Durkheim on Institutional Analysis*. Chicago: University of Chicago Press, 1978.

Ehrlich, Isaac. "The Deterrent Effect of Capital Punishment: A Question of Life and Death." *American Economic Review* (1975) 65:397.

Ellsworth, Phoebe C. and Lee Ross. "Public Opinion and Judicial Decision Making: An Example from Research on Capital Punishment."

In Hugo Adam Bedau and Chester M. Pierce, eds., *Capital Punishment in the United States*. New York: AMS Press, 1976.

Engels, Friedrich. *Anti-Dühring*. London: Lawrence and Wishart, 1943.

—— *The Condition of the Working Class in England*. Oxford: B. Blackwell, 1958.

Erskine, Hazel. "The Polls: Capital Punishment." *Public Opinion Quarterly* (November 1970) 34:290.

Esmain, A. *Histoire de la procédure criminelle en France*. Paris: Larose et Forcel, 1882.

Figlio, Robert M. "The Seriousness of Offenses: An Evaluation by Offenders and Non-Offenders." *J. of Criminal Law and Criminology* (1975) 66:189.

Filler, Louis. "Movements to Abolish the Death Penalty in the United States." *Annals of the American Academy of Political and Social Science* (November 1952) 284:124.

Frankel, David S. "The Constitutionality of the Mandatory Death Penalty for Life-Term Prisoners Who Murder." *New York Univ. L. R.* (1980) 55:636.

Freudenthal, Berthold. "Antworten, Griechisch." In Theodor Mommsen, *Zum ältesten Strafrecht der Kulturvölker*. Leipzig: Duncker and Humblot, 1905.

Freund, Paul A. *The Supreme Court of the United States*. Cleveland: Meridian Books, 1961.

Friedman, Lawrence M. *A History of American Law*. New York: Simon and Shuster, 1973.

Garçon, E. *Le droit pénal, origines, évolution, etat actuel*. Paris: Payot, 1922.

Glueck, Sheldon and Eleanor Glueck. *Unraveling Juvenile Delinquency*. Cambridge, Mass.: Harvard University Press, 1951.

Goldberg, Arthur J. and Alan M. Dershowitz. "Declaring the Death Penalty Unconstitutional." *Harvard L. R.* (1970) 83:1773.

Goldschmidt, Walter. *Man's Way—A Preface to the Understanding of Human Society*. Cleveland: World Publishing Company, 1959.

Gorecki, Jan. "Crime Causation Theories—Failures and Perspectives." *British J. of Sociology* (1974) 25/4:461.

—— "Leon Petrażycki." In Jan Gorecki, ed., *Sociology and Jurisprudence of Leon Petrażycki*. Urbana, Ill.: University of Illinois Press, 1975.

—— "Moral Premises of Contemporary Divorce Laws." In J. Ekelaar and S. Katz, eds., *Family Living in a Changing Society*. Toronto: Butterworth, 1980.

—— "Recrimination in Eastern Europe." *American J. of Comparative Law* (1966) 14:617.

—— A *Theory of Criminal Justice*. New York: Columbia University Press, 1979.

Gottlieb, Gerald H. "Testing the Death Penalty." *So. Cal. L. R.* (1961) 34:264.

Gwiazdomorski, Jan. *Prawo spadkowe* [*Law of Inheritance*]. Warsaw: Panstwowe Wydawnictwo Naukowe, 1959.

Hälschner, Hugo. *Das Preussische Strafrecht*, 1 Teil: *Geschichte des Brandenburgisch-Preussischen Strafrechts*. Bonn, 1855.

Hammond, N. G. L. A *History of Greece to 322 B.C.* Oxford: Clarendon Press, 1959.

Harrison, A. R. W. *The Law of Athens*. Oxford: Clarendon Press, 1971.

Hatzfield, Jean. *History of Ancient Greece*. Edinburgh: Oliver and Boyd, 1966.

Heline, Theodore. *Capital Punishment*. Los Angeles: New Age Press, 1965.

Hempel, Carl G. *Aspects of Scientific Explanation*, New York: The Free Press, 1965.

Heumann, Milton. *Plea Bargaining*. Chicago: University of Chicago Press, 1977.

Hippel, Robert V. *Deutsches Strafrecht*. Berlin: Julius Springer Verlag, 1925.

Hood, Roger and Richard Sparks. "Citizens' Attitudes and Police Practice in Reporting Offenses." In Israel Drapkin and Emilio Viano, eds., *Victimology*. Lexington, Mass.: Lexington Books, 1974.

Horowitz, Elinor L. *Capital Punishment, U.S.A.* Philadelphia: J. B. Lippincott, 1973.

Howard, John. *The State of the Prisons in England and Wales with Some Preliminary Observations and an Account of Some Foreign Prisons*. Warrington England: W. Eyres, 1777.

Jolowicz, H. F. and Barry Nicholas. *Historical Introduction to the Study of Roman Law*. Cambridge, England: Cambridge University Press, 1972.

Jones, A. H. M. *The Criminal Courts of the Roman Republic and the Principate*. Oxford: Basil Blackwell, 1972.

Jones, J. Walter. *The Law and Legal Theory of the Greeks*. Oxford: Oxford University Press, 1956.

Klein, Lawrence B., Brian Frost, and Victor Filatov. "The Deterrent Effect of Capital Punishment: An Assessment of the Evidence." In Hugo Adam Bedau, ed., *The Death Penalty in America*. Oxford: Oxford University Press, 1982.

Köhler, W. *The Mentality of Apes*. New York: Harcourt Brace, 1925.

Kotarbiński, Tadeusz. *Gnosiology*. Oxford: Pergamon Press, 1966.

Kunkel, Wolfgang. *An Introduction to Roman Legal and Constitutional History*. Oxford: Oxford University Press, 1966.

—— *Untersuchungen zur Entwicklung des Römischen Kriminalverfahrens in vorsullanischer Zeit*. München: Bayerische Akademie der Wissenschaften, 1952.

Lande, Jerzy. "The Sociology of Petrażycki." In Jan Gorecki, ed., *Sociology and Jurisprudence of Leon Petrażycki*. Urbana, Ill.: University of Illinois Press 1975.

—— *Studia z filozofii prawa* [*Studies in Philosophy of Law*]. Warszawa: Panstwowe Wydawnictwo Naukowe, 1959.

Latte, Kurt. "Beiträge zum Griechischen Strafrecht." In Erich Berneker, ed., *Zur Griechischen Rechtsgeschichte*. Darmstadt: Wissenschaftliche Buchgesellschaft, 1968.

Lenin, Vladimir I. *State and Revolution*. New York: International Publishers, 1932.

Linden, David R. "Transfer of Approach Responding Between Punishment, Frustrative Nonreward, and the Combination of Punishment and Nonreward." *Learning and Motivation* (1974) 5:498.

Lummus, Henry T. *The Trial Judge*. Chicago: Foundation Press, 1937.

MacDowell, Douglas M. *Athenian Homicide Law*. Manchester, England: Manchester University Press, 1963.

—— *The Law in Classical Athens*. Ithaca, N.Y.: Cornell University Press, 1978.

Mackey, Philip English. "The Inutility of Mandatory Capital Punishment: An Historical Note." *Boston Univ. L. R.* (1974) 54:32.

—— *Voices Against Death*. New York: Burt Franklin, 1976.

Martin, Barclay. "Reward and Punishment Associated with the Same Goal Response." *Psychological Bulletin* (1963) 5:441.

Martinson, Robert. "What Works? Questions and Answers About Prison Reform." *The Public Interest* (1974) 35:22.

Marx, Karl. "Preface to the Critique of Political Economy." In Karl Marx and Frederick Engels. *Selected Works*. Moscow: Foreign Languages Pub. House, 1962, vol. 1.

McCord, William, Joan McCord, and Irving Kenneth Zola. *Origins of Crime*. New York: Columbia University Press, 1959.

Meltsner, Michael. *Cruel and Unusual*. New York: Random House, 1973.

Merle, Roger and André Vitu. *Traité de droit criminel*. Paris, édition Cujas, 1967.

Merton, Robert K. *Social Theory and Social Structure*. New York: Free Press, 1968.

Mitford, Jessica. *Kind and Usual Punishment*. New York: Vintage Books, 1973.

Moley, Raymond. "The Vanishing Jury." *So. Cal. L. R.* (1928) 2/2:97.

Mommsen, Theodor. *Römisches Strafrecht*. Leipzig: Duncker & Humbolt, 1899.

Montesquieu. *The Spirit of Laws*. London: J. Nourse and P. Vaillant, 1773 (Thomas Nugent' translation).

Newman, Donald J. *Conviction—The Determination of Guilt or Innocence Without Trial*. Boston: Little, Brown, 1966.

Note: "Discretion and the Constitutionality of the New Death Penalty Statutes." *Harvard L.R.* (1974) 87:1690.

Ossowska, Maria. *Social Determinants of Moral Ideas*. London: Routledge and Kegan Paul, 1971.

Parke, Ross D. "The Role of Punishment in the Socialization Process." In Ronald A. Hoppe, G. Alexander Milton, and Edward S. Simmel, eds., *Early Experiences in the Process of Socialization*. New York: Academic Press, 1970.

Parke, Ross D., J. L. Deur, and D. B. Sawin. "The Intermittent Punishment Effect in Humans: Conditioning or Adaptation?" *Psychonomic Science* (1970) 18:193.

Passell, Peter. "The Deterrent Effect of the Death Penalty: A Statistical Test." *Stanford L. R.* (1975) 28:61.

Passell, Peter and John B. Taylor. "The Deterrent Effect of Capital Punishment: Another View." *American Economic Review* (June 1977) 67/3:445.

Petrażycki, Leon. *Law and Morality*. Cambridge, Mass.: Harvard University Press, 1955.

——— *Wstęp do nauki polityki prawa* [Introduction to the Science of Legal Policy]. Warszawa: Panstwowe Wydawnictwo Naukowe, 1968.

——— *Teoriia prava i gosudarstva v sviazi s teoriei nravstvennosti* [Theory of Law and State in Connection with a Theory of Morality]. vol. 2. St. Petersburg: Ekateringofskoe Pechatnoe Delo, 1910.

Plutarch's Lives (Perrin's translation), vol. 1, *Solon XVII*. Cambridge, Mass.: Harvard University Press, 1948.

Podgórecki, Adam. *Law and Society*. London: Routledge & Kegan Paul, 1974.

——— "Unrecognized Father of Sociology of Law: Leon Petrażycki." *Law and Society Review* (1980) 15:183.

Pollock, Frederick and Frederic William Maitland. *The History of Eng-*

lish Law, vol. 2. Cambridge, England: Cambridge University Press, 1899.

Popper, Karl R. *The Open Society and Its Enemies*. Princeton, N.J.: Princeton University Press, 1966.

President's Commission on Law Enforcement and Administration of Justice. *The Challenge of Crime in a Free Society*. Washington, D.C.: U.S. Government Printing Office, 1967.

President's Commission on Law Enforcement and Administration of Justice. *Task Force Report: The Courts*. Washington, D.C.: U.S. Government Printing Office, 1967.

Radbruch, Gustav. *Rechtsphilosophie*. Stuttgart: K. F. Koehler Verlag, 1963.

Radin, Jane Margaret. "Cruel Punishment and Respect for Persons: Super Due Process for Death." *So. Cal. L. R.* (1980) 53:1143.

Radzinowicz, Leon. *A History of English Criminal Law*, vol. 1. New York: Macmillan, 1948.

Riedel, Marc. "Discrimination in the Imposition of the Death Penalty: A Comparison of the Characteristics of Offenders Sentenced Pre-*Furman* and Post-*Furnam*." *Temple L. Q.* (1976) 49:261.

Rosett, Arthur and Donald R. Cressey. *Justice by Consent*. Philadelphia: J. B. Lippincott Company, 1976.

Rossi, Peter H., Emily Waite, Christine E. Bose, and Richard E. Berk. "The Seriousness of Crimes: Normative Structure and Individual Differences." *American Sociological Review* (1974) 39:224.

Rostovtzeff, M. *A History of the Ancient World*. Oxford: Clarendon Press, 1926.

Royal Commission on Capital Punishment. *Report*. London: Her Majesty's Stationery Office, 1953.

Rubin, Sol. *The Law of Criminal Correction*. St. Paul, Minn.: West, 1973.

—— "The Supreme Court, Cruel and Unusual Punishment, and the Death Penalty." *Crime and Delinquency* (January 1969) 15:121.

Sabatier, A. "Napoléon et les codes criminels." *Revue pénitentiaire et de droit pénal*, 1910, p. 905.

Salmonowicz, Stanislaw. *Prawo karne oświeconego absolutyzmu* [*Criminal Law of the Enlightened Despotism*]. Torun: Towarzystwo Naukowe w Toruniu, 1966.

Schulhofer, S. "Harm and Punishment: A Critique of Emphasis on the Results of Conduct in the Criminal Law." *Penn. L. R.* (1974) 122:1497.

Sears, Robert R., Eleanor E. Maccoby, and Harry Levin. *Patterns of Child Rearing*. White Plains, N.Y.: Row, Peterson, 1957.

Sellin, Thorsten. "Homicides in Retentionist and Abolitionist States." In Thorsten Sellin, ed., *Capital Punishment*. New York: Harper and Row, 1967.

Spear, Charles. *Essays on the Punishment of Death*. Boston, 1844.

Spitzer, Steven. "Punishment and Social Organization: A Study of Durkheim's Theory of Penal Evolution." *Law and Society Review* (1975) 9:614.

Stefani, Gaston and Georges Lavasseur. *Droit pénal général et procédure pénale*. Paris: Librarie Dalloz, 1972.

Stephen, James Fitzjames. *A History of the Criminal Law of England*, vol. I. London: Macmillan, 1883.

Stinchcombe, Arthur L. and Associates. *Crime and Punishment—Changing Attitudes in America*. San Francisco: Jossey-Bass, 1980.

Strachan-Davidson, James Leigh. *Problems of the Roman Criminal Law*. Oxford: Clarendon Press, 1912.

Thomas, Charles W. "Eighth Amendment Challenges to the Death Penalty: The Relevance of Informed Public Opinion." *Vanderbilt L. R.* (1977) 30:1005.

Thomas, Charles W. and Samuel G. Foster. "A Sociological Perspective on Public Support for Capital Punishment." *Amer. J. of Orthopsychiatry* (1975) 45/4:641.

Thomas, Charles W. and Robert G. Howard. "Public Attitudes Toward Capital Punishment—A Comparative Analysis." *Journal of Behavioral Economics* (1977) 6:189.

United States Senate. *To Abolish the Death Penalty*. Hearings before the Subcommittee on Criminal Laws and Procedures. Washington, D.C.: U.S. Government Printing Office, 1970.

Van den Haag, Ernest. *Punishing Criminals*. New York: Basic Books, 1975.

Vidmar, Neil and Phoebe Ellsworth. "Public Opinion and the Death Penalty." *Stanford L. R.* (1974) 26:1245.

Wagner, Allan R. "Frustration and Punishment." In Ralph Norman Haber, ed., *Current Research in Motivation*. New York: Holt, Rinehart and Winston, 1966, pp. 229.

Wertheimer, Alan. Book Review. *American J. of Sociology* (1981) 86:1169.

Wilson, James Q. *Thinking About Crime*. New York: Basic Books, 1975.

The Wolfenden Report. New York: Stein and Day, 1963.

Wolfgang, Marvin E. and Marc Riedel. "Race, Racial Discrimination and the Death Penalty." *Annals of the American Academy of Political and Social Science* (1973) 407:119.

Zimring, Franklin E. and Gordon J. Hawkins. *Deterrence.* Chicago: University of Chicago Press, 1973.

Zimring, Franklin E., Sheila O'Malley, and Joel Eigen. "The Going Price of Criminal Homicide in Philadelphia." *Chicago L.R.* (1976) 43:277.

INDEX

Abolition or near abolition: in various states in the U.S., 3, 86, 91, 93, 123*nn*1 and 2, 141–42*n*50; in England, 4, 62–63; in Rome, 48; in Australia, 56; in Germany, 57; in France, 60

Abolitionist campaign: in Germany, 57; in England, 62; in the U.S., 84–85, 87–90

Abolitionist ideas: sanctity of life, 4, 85, 88; danger of executing the innocent, 4, 7, 85, 87–88; deterrence, 4, 6–7, 8, 85, 88; suffering of convicts, 4, 7, 85, 88; rehabilitation, 4, 7, 85, 89–90; social determinants of criminal behavior, 4, 89; arbitrariness of executions, 4, 6, 7; demoralizing impact of capital punishment, 4, 7, 85; and the Supreme Court, 5–8, 90, 93–95, 123*n*11, 123–24*n*13, 124–25*nn*17 and 18; human dignity, 6; abhorrent harshness of capital punishment, 6–7, 85, 88; purposelessness of capital punishment, 6–7; inequality and discrimination, 7, 9, 10, 16, 89, 90; merciful acquittals, 88–89; personality of retentionists, 147*n*59; *see also* Retentionist ideas

Abolitionists in the U.S., 3–4, 83–95; as a traditional minority, 3; on the increase, 3, 91, 97; organized, 3, 84–85, 87; nearly winning, 4, 93–95, 143*n*52; aggressive tactics of, 92–93; on the decrease, 97, 108–10, 111–12; *see also* Retentionist sentiment in the U.S.

Absolute responsibility, 68–9

Amsel, A., 67–8

Amsterdam, Anthony, 92

Ancel, Marc, 135–36*n*108

Anger about crime, in the U.S.: and increase of punitive attitudes, 28, 108–10, 119, 147*n*58; and decline of abolitionist sentiment, 97, 109–10; reasons for, 106–7; rising, 109–10; and reform of criminal justice system, 119; as a dubious cue for policy, 119–20; *see also* Fear of crime

Appelate review of death sentences: automatic, after *Furman*, 26, 129*n*33; in Rome, 47, 133*n*56; aggressive, preceding *Furman*, 92

Arbitrariness: in imposing the death penalty, 4, 6, 7, 9–10, 12–13; and cruelty of punishment, 6, 124–25*n*17; and prejudice, 7, 10, 16; pervading criminal justice system, 11–13, 102–105; and plea bargaining, 12, 20, 103–5; inherent in the sentencing process, 21–24; and discretion, 9–10, 11–13, 102–5, 124*n*17; *see also* Discretion, Guidance in discretion, Justice and injustice

Athens: decline of punitive harshness, 35, 38–42, 132*n*28; development of knowledge, 36–37; development of arts, 37; socialization, 37–38; political progress, 37–38; plea bargaining, 132*n*28; *see also* Draco's code, Pericles, Solon

Augustus: the peak of Roman civilization, 42, 45; political system of Rome, 42, 45; *Pax Romana*, 44